STRATEGIC PLANNING FOR CHURCH AND MINISTRY

R. HENRY MIGLIORE, PH.D.

President, Managing for Success Professor Emeritus NSU/UCT

Managing for Success

Tulsa, Oklahoma

Strategic Planning for Church and Ministry
978-0-9989006-4-3

Copyright © 2018 by R. Henry Migliore

Published by
Managing for Success
10839 S. Houston
Jenks, Oklahoma 74037
www.hmigliore.com

Table of Contents

Chapter 1
Biblical Perspectives of Planning..1
  Planning Is Important 1
  What Is Planning? 3
  Types of Plans... 4
  Advantages of Planning for Churches and Ministries 4
  Planning's Place in the Church or Ministry................................... 7
  The Greatest Needs of Today's Ministries and Churches 10
  Summary... 12
  References 14

Chapter 2
Overview of Strategic Planning 15
  What Is Strategic Planning? 15
  The Strategic Planning Process 15
  Analysis and Assumptions.. 19
  Establishing Objectives 20
  Strategy Development 20
  Operational Plans.. 21
  Evaluation and Control... 21
  Strategic Planning as a Process 22
  Strategy Implementation 22
  Summary... 23
  Planning Process Worksheet... 23
  References 25

Chapter 3
Defining Your Purpose 27
  The Importance of Defining Purpose.. 27
  Writing a Statement of Purpose 28
  Sample Mission Statements... 29
  Evaluating A Purpose Statement.. 34
  Summary... 36
  Purpose Statement Worksheet 36
  References 37

Chapter 4
Analysis and Assumptions 39
  External Analysis.. 39
  Assessing Opportunities and Threats 40
  Internal Analysis.. 41
  Assessing Strengths and Weaknesses 42
  Making Assumptions 43
  Summary... 45

Analysis and Assumptions Worksheet 45
References 46

Chapter 5
Establishing Objectives **47**
Nature and Role of Objectives...47
Alternatives to Managing by Objectives 48
Characteristics of Good Objectives 49
Types of Objectives Included in a Strategic Plan..53
Using Environmental Analysis Data to Set Objectives 56
Overall Church Objectives, 1996-1998 57
Review Sheet Management Plan, 1996 60
Church Administrator's Objectives, 1996 60
Summary...61
Objectives Worksheet 62
References 63

Chapter 6
Developing Strategy and Operational Plans **65**
Strategy Concepts 65
Alternate Strategies..65
Factors Influencing the Strategy Selected 67
Operational Plans...68
Summary...72
Strategy Development Worksheet 73

Chapter 7
Evaluation and Control Procedures **75**
Integration of Planning and Control 75
Performance Evaluation and Control 77
Establishing Procedures...79
Performance Evaluation Guidelines 80
Summary...80
Evaluation and Control Worksheet 80

Appendix A
Church and Ministry Strategic and Management Planning Worksheets.....**83**
Set Up A Way To Monitor How You Are Doing & A Way
To Create Action 86
Action Plan Objective: 87

Appendix B:
Church Ministry: Strategic Marketing Plan **89**
Church/Ministry Strategic Marketing Plan to Support the Church/Ministry Overall
Marketing Plan 89
General Marketing Strategy 89

Appendix C:

Strategic Plan: Calvary Temple of Temple Terrace......................**95**
   Purpose 95
   Objectives and Goals...98
   Revised General Strategies..98
   Calvary Temple Administrative and Operational Structure.......................99

Appendix D:
Strategic Plan: Inner City Marketing Plan **103**
   Strategic Objective 103
   GMCC Background 103
   Environmental Analysis 103
   Church Organization Chart.......................................104
   Strengths 104
   Objectives & Goals 104
   Administrative & Operational Structure 105
   Marketing Plan 106
   Key Market Segments 112
   Financial Forecast 113
   Human Resources Plan 117
   Action Plan 119

Appendix E
Planning, Organization, and Common Sense
Leadership with a Biblical Perspective.............................**121**
   Case Study: Things Got Out of Whack at the Church....................121
     Individual Planning Seminar Worksheet..........................124
   How Big: A Plan or Accident?................................126
     Conclusion 130
   When Does the Holy Spirit Take Over and Strategy End?..............130
   Biblically Based Analysis of Planning and Management Principles.........133
     Conclusion 139
     References...139
   Common Sense Management. A Biblical Perspective..................140

About the Author **149**

Index..**151**

Chapter 1
Biblical Perspectives of Planning

> *Commit to the LORD whatever you do, and your plans will*
> *succeed.*
> —*Proverbs 16:3*

If you are struggling with any of the following problems or questions, this book, Church and Ministry Strategic Planning, may be very important to you.

Why is there so much confusion among our associate pastors on what we are trying to accomplish?

Why is there so much dissension and disagreement in this church?

Why is there such a high turnover of people in our church, especially in leadership positions?

Why did we build that building when it is not being used? As a pastor, why am I working 12 hours a day, and can never keep up?

Why have we failed on a number of projects and missions? Why did God let us down?

Why is the Devil stopping us?

Why have the elders asked me to resign after everything I have put into this church or ministry?

Why does this church lack enthusiasm?

If you are wrestling with one of these questions, the answer might be that your church or ministry lacks good long-term strategic planning. Part of strategic planning is the team building approach of developing leaders and involving people in the plan.

Planning Is Important

Planning as part of the management process is crucial to the success of any organization. This is especially true for the Church, although little research has been done on the relationship of planning to successful church ministry. Recently, however, an empirical study of the relationship between the use of the planning process and ministry effectiveness was conducted among senior pastors in one denomination. The study found that

- Larger churches (congregations of 250 or more) are more inclined to engage in written long-range planning;

- Most churches had been using long-range planning for less than three years and achieved attendance increases of 100 percent, twice the growth rate experienced by churches not using long-range planning;
- Ministry effectiveness was increased by the presence of written yearly and long-range plans;
- The lack of a written plan (yearly and/or long-range) hindered the ability of the church/pastor to be effective in ministering to the community.

The most important conclusion, according to the author of this research study, is that:

> *Pastors and church leaders must be taught the importance of utilizing administration and management skills, especially planning, in the Church. They must also be given the tools necessary to incorporate planning into the ministries of the churches they serve. It is only through prayer and the use of the planning process that the Church, as an organization, can effectively fulfill the Great Commission that it has been given (Burns 1992).*

Of a large number of decisions made by a church or by an individual pastor, there are a handful that can significantly impact the future of the church or pastor. These strategic decisions require careful identification and thoughtful consideration. This is the nature of the role of strategic planning.

Perspectives of strategic thinking can be illustrated with this question: Who are the two most important persons responsible for the success of an airplane's flight? Typical responses would be

- the pilot and the navigator,
- the pilot and the maintenance supervisor,
- the pilot and the air traffic controller, or
- the pilot and the flight engineer.

All of these responses recognize the day-to-day hands-on importance of the pilot, and they all introduce one of several other important support or auxiliary functionaries to the answer. However, each of these segmented responses ignores the one person who is perhaps the single most important individual to the ultimate success of the airplane—the designer. The pilot and the designer are perhaps the two most important individuals to the success of an airplane: the pilot because of his day-to-day responsibilities in commanding the craft, and the designer because of his ability to create a concept that can be economically constructed, easily operated by any normally competent flight crew, and maintained safely by the ground crew.

Most contemporary pastors perceive themselves as the "pilot" of the church: taking off, landing, conferring with the navigator, and communicating with the air traffic controller. They generally view themselves as the chief hands-on operational manager.

However, what has been most lacking in churches and ministries in the past few years has been an appreciation for the strategic viewpoint. There is a need for more emphasis on the "designer's" approach to operating a church or ministry. A well-conceived strategic planning system can facilitate this emphasis.

In a similar analogy, consider the illustration offered in the book, The Master Builder (Benjamin, Durkin, and Iverson 1985, in which church strategic planning and flying are compared. The authors note that before radios and instruments became common in small planes, pilots had to fly by visual flight rules. This meant that after takeoff the plane had to be oriented in the right direction by some visual landmarks, perhaps a mountain that could be seen 50 miles out on the horizon. By keeping their eyes fixed on that landmark, the pilots could keep the plane steady and moving straight toward a long-range destination. A plane's magnetic compass needle would tend to sway, causing the plane to swerve back and forth in a wide zig-zag pattern. It could not provide steady direction because of its shortened gyrations. A pilot who tried to follow it strictly might never reach the destination, especially if fuel was limited.

This analogy clearly illustrates the difference between a short- and long-term perspective: one is choppy, erratic, and wastes fuel; the other guides the plane on a steady, constant, and certain course. A church without a long-term planning perspective faces the same situation. Instead of moving steadily toward God's goals, it will continually swerve off course due to the endless distractions that can prevent a church from pursuing God's purpose and vision. Thus, strategic planning is one of the keys to success of any undertaking and nowhere is it more important than in churches and ministries.

What Is Planning?

Planning may be defined as a managerial activity, which involves analyzing the environment, setting objectives, deciding on specific actions needed to reach the objectives, and also providing feedback on results. This process should be distinguished from the plan itself, which is a written document containing the results of the planning process; it is a written statement of what is to be done and how it is to be done. Planning is a continuous process, which both precedes and follows other functions, in which plans are made and executed, and results are used to make new plans as the process continues.

Types of Plans

There are many types of plans but most can be categorized as strategic or tactical. Strategic plans cover a long period of time and may be referred to as a long-term plan. They are broad in scope and basically answer the question of how an organization is to commit its resources over the next five to ten years. Strategic plans are altered on an infrequent basis to reflect changes in the environment or overall direction of the ministry.

Tactical plans cover a short time period, usually a year or less. They are often referred to as short-term or operational plans. They specify what is to be done in a given year to move the organization toward its long-term objectives. In other words, what we do this year (short term) needs to be tied to where we want to be five to ten years in the future (long term).

Most churches and ministries, which have been involved in planning, have focused on short-term rather than long-term planning. Although this is better than not planning at all, it also means each year's plan is not related to anything long-term in nature and usually fails to move the organization to where it wants to be in the future.

Programs and events require planning. A ministry program is a large set of activities involving a whole area of a church's capabilities, such as planning for a church day school program. Planning for programs involves:

1.   Dividing the total set of activities into meaningful parts;

2.   Assigning planning responsibility for each part to appropriate people;

3.   Assigning target dates for completion of plans;

4.   Determining and allocating the resources needed for each part.

Each major program or division within a church or ministry should have a strategic plan in place to provide a blueprint for the program over time.

A ministry event is generally of less scope and complexity. It is also not likely to be repeated on a regular basis. An event may be a part of a broader program or it may be self-contained. Even though it is a one-time event, planning is essential to accomplishing the objectives of the project and coordinating the activities, which make up the event. A plan to have a "friend day" would be an example of a project plan.

Advantages of Planning for Churches and Ministries

Why should a church or ministry devote time to planning?
Consider the following questions:

•   Do you know where you are going and how you are going to get there?

•   Does everyone know what you are trying to accomplish?

- Do all those involved know what is expected of them?

If the answer to any of these is no, then your church or ministry needs to develop a long-range plan with as many people involved as possible. Alvin J. Lindgren observed that:

> *Most churches do not engage in such systematic long-range planning. Perhaps this is one reason why the church has not been able to reach and change society more effectively. Many churches operate on hand-to-mouth planning. They consider the pressing problems of the moment at each board meeting without placing them in proper perspective in relationship to either past or future (1965, 226).*

In many small churches, pastors may object to planning, thinking that it makes no sense for them, since theirs is only a small organization and everyone in the congregation knows what happened in the past year and what is likely to happen in the coming year. Another frequent objection is that there is no time for planning. A third is that there are not enough resources to allow for planning. All of these objections actually point out the necessity for planning even in the small church. Such an organization may actually have a sizeable budget, making it imperative to have a plan of where the church is heading. The observation that there is no time for planning may seem accurate, but this is probably due to the lack of planning in the past, which has left insufficient time for attention to such necessities. Finally, the argument that there are insufficient resources actually justifies the role of planning in order to obtain the maximum benefit from those resources being used in the church or ministry. Thus, planning is a critical element in any church's success.

Planning has many advantages. For example, it helps church or ministry administrators to adapt to changing environments, take advantage of opportunities, created by change, reach agreements on major issues, and place responsibility more precisely. It also gives a sense of direction to staff members as well as providing a basis for gaining their commitment. The sense of vision that can be provided in a well-written plan also instills a sense of loyalty in church or ministry members or constituents.

A church can benefit from the planning process because this systematic, continuing process allows it to:

1. Assess the church's market position. This involves what is termed a SWOT analysis—examining the church's internal Strengths and Weaknesses and external Opportunities and Threats. Without explicit planning, these elements may go unrecognized.

2. Establish goals, objectives, priorities, and strategies to be completed within specified time periods.

3.   Assess accomplishment of the goals that are set and will help motivate staff and members to work together to achieve shared goals.

4.   Achieve greater staff and member commitment and teamwork aimed at meeting challenges and solving problems presented by changing conditions.

5.   Muster its resources to meet these changes through anticipation and preparation. "Adapt or die" is a very accurate admonition.

Pastors cannot control the future, but they should attempt to identify and isolate present actions and forecast how results can be expected to influence the future. The primary purpose of planning, then, is to ensure that current programs can be used to increase the chances of achieving future objectives and goals; that is, to increase the chances of making better decisions today that affect tomorrow's performance.

Unless planning leads to improved performance, it is not worthwhile. Thus, to have a church or ministry that looks forward to the future and tries to stay alive and prosper in a changing environment, there must be active, vigorous, continuous, and creative planning. Otherwise, a church will only react to its environment.

There are basically two reasons for planning: (1) protective benefits resulting from reduced chances for error in decision making, and (2) positive benefits, in the form of increased success in reaching ministry objectives.

Often, when pastors and churches plan poorly, they must constantly devote their energies to solving problems that would not have existed, or at least would be much less serious, with planning. They spend their time fighting fires rather than practicing fire prevention.

Long-range planning can become a means of renewal in the life of a congregation if the following points are remembered:

1.   A unified purpose can be achieved only when all segments of the life of the church see themselves as part of a larger whole with a single goal;

2.   Isolated individual decisions and commitments often influence future plans, even when they are not intended to do so;

3.   When careful planning is lacking, groups in the church often become competitive and duplicate one another's work;

4.   Without coordinated planning, groups in the church may come to feel they are ends in themselves and lose their sense of perspective in relation to the church;

5.   Long-range planning is demanded by the magnitude of each church's task (Lindgren 1965, 231).

Planning's Place in the Church or Ministry

All pastors engage in planning to some degree. As a general rule, the larger the church becomes, the more the primary planning activities become associated with groups of people as opposed to individuals.

Many larger churches develop a planning committee or staff.

Organizations set up such a planning group for one or more of the following reasons:

1. Planning takes time. A planning group can reduce the work-load of individual staff or members.

2. Planning takes coordination. A planning group can help integrate and coordinate the planning activities of individual staff.

3. Planning takes expertise. A planning group can bring to a particular problem more tools and techniques than any single individual.

4. Planning takes objectivity. A planning group can take a broader view than one individual and go beyond specific projects and particular church departments.

A planning group generally has three basic areas of responsibility. First, it assists the pastor in developing goals, policies, and strategies for the church. The group facilitates the planning process by scanning and monitoring the church's environment. A second major responsibility of the group is to coordinate the planning of different levels and units within the church. Finally the planning group acts as an organizational resource for pastors who lack expertise in planning.

In smaller churches, planning and execution must usually be carried out by the same people. The greatest challenge is to set aside time for planning in the midst of all the other day-to-day activities.

Resistance To The Planning Process

There are three main reasons why planning does not get done in churches and ministries today: (1) pastors and members lack training, (2) many perceive it as unscriptural, and (3) problems in implementation.

Lack of Management Training

The majority of churches in the United States have fewer than 200 active members, according to the data available from major denominations (Boyce 1984, 96). Most pastors have minimal management education and experience before entering active ministry and want to spend their time performing pastoral functions for which they are trained. Furthermore, few of these churches can or do draw on a pool of lay people with management training or skills. As such, the planning, objective setting, and other management functions are largely neglected.

Planning is Thought to be Unscriptural

Planning and objective setting of the strategic type have been largely neglected or purposely avoided by churches. This reluctance to plan stems from the fact that many view the application of strategic planning as inappropriate and nonspiritual (Van Auken and Johnson 1984, 85). Some have felt that because churches are not businesses, they must not be managed as such: spiritual management is required for a spiritual organization. According to this view, church leaders are supposed to manage through God's perfect guidance and direction, to wait patiently for God to make things happen rather than forcing things to happen. Furthermore, churches are admonished to strive for truly spiritual goals, not the numerical or quantifiable goals stressed in business.

Although planning has received more and more recognition for its applicability to churches, there are still some who doubt its worth to a religious organization.

For example, a pastor may be ridiculed by some for setting numeric goals, as this may not seem to be "religious." Often it is believed that the pastor is taking on the world's standards if he operates using business skills that have been applied to the secular world. But the same pastor may have no second thoughts about using the same type of sound system used by a business or even a rock band. A sound system is not good or bad in itself but rather the issue is how it is used. Planning which moves the church away from God's call is just bad planning; but planning as an activity is not bad in itself. The same can be said of money. The love of money is the root of all evil, not money itself.

A careful study of the Bible demonstrates the appropriateness and necessity for believers to plan their daily affairs. What does the Bible say about planning? We believe the Holy Spirit helps us know God's will and actions that are anointed. We do our best, then ask God for His best. Our spirit confirms when the right plan is in the will of God. Nothing in this book is meant to imply that the Lord is to be left out. Remember that a church's master plan should be the Master's plan for that church. Consider the following Bible verses:

> *Suppose one of you wants to build a tower. Will he not first sit down and estimate the cost to see if he has enough money to complete it?—Luke 14:28*

> *But everything should be done in a fitting and orderly way.—1 Corinthians 14:40*

> *Commit to the Lord whatever you do, and your plans will succeed.—Proverbs 16:3*

In his heart a man plans his course,. but the Lord determines his steps.—Proverbs 16:9

May he give you the desire of your heart and make all your' plans succeed.—Psalm 20:4

Whatever you do, work at it with all your heart, as working for the Lord, not for men.—Colossians 3:23

Plans fail for lack of counsel, but with many advisers they succeed.—Proverbs 15:22

The purposes of a man's heart are deep waters, but a man of understanding draws them out.—Proverbs 20:5

By wisdom a house is built, and through understanding it is established.—Proverbs 24:3

For God is not a God of disorder but of peace.—1 Corinthians 14:33

In Appendix A we provide additional Bible verses related to planning.

Implementation Problems

Although there is much academic and theoretical support for planning, the actual implementation of it often runs aground on the shores of ministry reality. Even among very progressive churches you find significant resistance to planning. Some of the most common arguments against it are:

1. Planning is not action oriented;

2. Planning takes too much time, we are too busy to plan;

3. Planning is unrealistic because of the rapid change in our environment (demographics,. etc.);

4. Planning becomes an end, not just a means to an end.

Many of these arguments stem from the same kind of thinking that would rank the pilot as the most important person in the success of an airplane. To be helpful, planning does not depend on complete forecasting accuracy. In fact, a variety of futuristic alternatives or scenarios can be very helpful in establishing planning parameters. Often a best, most likely, and worst case approach is used. This three-level forecast gives dimension to the process of recognizing, anticipating, and managing change.

The objection that planning is not "hands-on" and related to the important day-to-day operations of the church is frequent. However, this point of view is shortsighted in terms of long-term success. Planning is not just for dreamers, in fact, it lets the church administrative team determine what can be done today to accomplish or avoid some future circumstance.

Planning sometimes becomes an end in the minds of some users. This is particularly true when planning is solely a committee responsibility within a church. A committee staff can facilitate the strategic planning process, but the process will not be a dynamic life-blood activity of the organization without the ongoing involvement of the pastor and staff members. President Eisenhower has been widely quoted as saying, "Plans are nothing, planning is everything." The trust he expressed was that the actual plan itself was not the end, but that the process of planning—developing futuristic scenarios, evaluating the environment and competition, assessing internal strengths and capabilities, and revising objectives and tactics was the organization dialogue that was most important. This church dialogue ideally breaks down barriers to communication, exposes blind spots, tests logic, measures the environment, and determines feasibility. The end result is more effective and efficient implementation of ministry activity.

Yet, the advantages of planning far outweigh any of these and other perceived disadvantages. Planning not only should be done but must be done.

The Greatest Needs of Today's Ministries and Churches

In our own informal surveys both denominational and nondenominational pastors appeared to be unanimous in their beliefs that strategic planning is important. To put matters into perspective, let us try to translate church and ministry success into a formula:

$$x = f(A,B,C,D,E,F,G,H,I \dots)$$

In this case x is success for the church or ministry, a dependent variable, and is on the left side of the equation. The = sign means a balance, or equal to what is on the other side; the f means "a function of." On the right side are all the independent variables that affect success:

A. Pastor as spiritual leader

B. Pastor as manager

C. Planning system

D. Organization system

E. Control system

F. Needs of people met

G. Denomination's national influence

H. Denomination's local influence

I. Location etc.

Only a few independent variables are listed, but the possibilities are endless. Notice that success is not necessarily equated to size. We are defining success in broader terms than church members, budget, and so forth. There seems to be a widespread notion that size is the only barometer, but we do not hold that belief.

God has raised up many spiritual leaders. We believe the greatest problems holding back these leaders—and the churches and ministries they serve—involve some combination of independent variables B, C, D, and E. Management, planning, organization, and control are some of the greatest needs of churches and ministries today.

We assume that every pastor is to some degree a spiritual leader or he could not remain in the pulpit. However, his entire ministry and the success of his church are in direct proportion to variables B, C, D, and E. If you assume all other variables are constant and full effort goes into B, C, D, and E, then the x factor (success), the dependent variable, has to increase. Without training and knowledge in the area of planning and management, the church and ministry have a ceiling on success. No organization can get any bigger than the capacity of its managers to manage. The hindrance is not the needs of the people, for needs are always there. It is not the denomination or location; it is plainly management, planning, organization, and control.

If pastors and evangelists could improve each of these areas just a little each year, they would be much more successful. They could drastically reduce all the obvious errors in direction, false starts, dissipated efforts, frustrated staff members, and waste. The religious world is ripe for criticism by almost anyone looking for waste and inefficiency.

Christians should not wait until someone comes along and creates a big scandal about waste and inefficiency. We need to put our shoulders to the wheel and pay attention to management, planning, organization, control, and people. If we do not, on the whole, the church will accomplish in the next 50 years about what it did in the last 50 years—it will maintain the status quo.

Our observation is that many people in ministry and church work are reluctant to plan, do not want a plan in writing, and do not ask for advice. The tendency is to be led by "the Spirit," which is sometimes a whim or emotional impulse. This reflects our general American inclination to "hang loose." Probably 75 percent of the profit-making organizations that we have observed or worked with have the same problem. The 25 percent that have the discipline to plan and manage properly far outperform those that do not. Higher profits, better service, and lower turnover are but a few of the rewards. The same good fortune comes to those ministries and churches that have the discipline to plan and manage properly.

Many times Christians say "The Devil is fighting us" when a plan or project goes sour. We are not discounting a demon force, but in many instances the Devil does not need to fight Christians. Could it be that we hold ourselves back? The Devil can sleep late and rest while we run around in circles. He does not need to work hard. We are our own worst enemies. Many church or ministry failures can be traced to poor planning, lack of getting people involved in the planning, and generally poor management. We often sense a spirit of extreme urgency in church ministry planning. This is used as a "go for it—if it is of the Lord, it will prosper" mentality. What is the rush? Many churches and ministries need to slow down, plan, and pray. Often they have rushed around in circles for the past few years. We do not believe God will give His best until we give our best. Included in doing our best is using the best planning and management philosophies and techniques available.

The need for the performance of managerial functions in churches in order for them to be more effective ministerially has long been recognized. Vast social questions and complex conditions in almost every community emphasize the need for good management in churches (Hale 1984, 30).

Where planning in churches occurs without quantitative goals, which are clearly understood and widely supported, vigorous progress is unlikely and probably impossible. The importance of setting goals is to provide direction and unity of purpose, but it must be the congregation's goal, as it is not the planners but the congregation that will ensure the plan's success. However, a balance should be struck and the two mistakes of planning extremes, those of asking the congregation to do either all the thinking or none, must be avoided. Planning is important to bring these objectives to fruition. This is not easy, but the alternative is for the church to be tossed to and fro, buffeted by every unforeseen circumstance, and blown off course.

We see creative planning as the church's hope for the future. Visionary thinking, solid purpose, or long-range dreams should be first in the basic concern of the church ministry. In a society where many institutions are becoming stagnant, it is imperative that churches have an expanding vision. Church planning has never been met with much enthusiasm. Even in larger churches, the enthusiasm for a plan seldom extends beyond a year unless it involves a new building. No matter how misunderstood and poorly appreciated planning is, it is a major factor in sharing the hope for the world—the gospel of Christ (McDonough 1975, 5).

Every pastor needs a vision or a dream. Mission statements and dreams are the vessels through which your desires are fulfilled. Without a specific goal, a vision is no vision.

Summary

We have attempted to establish in this chapter our belief that methods used successfully in industry are applicable to churches and ministries; (2) there is a place for better planning and management; (3) many pastors do believe that there is a need for planning; (4) most of the identifiable failures cannot be blamed on the Devil; and (5) the Bible supports, overall, a growing sense of the planning concept.

The philosophy of this book is that in order for everyone in the church or ministry—the elders, the pastor, the congregation—to be successful, a strategic plan is desperately needed. If you look at the mistakes of the past, it is obvious that many churches and ministries have followed the zig-zag flight pattern described earlier. Over years of consulting with churches and ministries, the authors have observed this exact pattern again and again. If you take the time and effort to study this book, follow up on your people, apply the format prescribed here, and prayerfully keep God in every step of the plan, here is what we believe you can expect:

1. A sense of enthusiasm in your church or ministry.

2. A five-year plan in writing to which everyone is committed.

3. A sense of commitment by the entire church to its overall direction.

4. Clear job duties and responsibilities.

5. Time for the leaders to do what they have been called to do.

6. Clear and evident improvement in the health and vitality of every member of the church staff.

7. Measurable improvement in the personal lives of all those in responsible positions with time for vacations, family, and personal pursuits.

8. The ability to measure very specifically the growth and contribution made by senior pastors or evangelists at the close of their careers.

9. Guaranteed leadership of the church or ministry because a plan is in place in writing and is understood—even more importantly, a management team and philosophy will be in place to guide the church or ministry into its next era of growth.

In the next chapter we present an overview of the entire strategic planning process; in Appendix B we also provide an outline of a strategic plan. Then, in the following chapters, we cover each step of the planning process. We explain the theory behind each step and give actual examples to help you to understand that step. Make notes on your own situation as you read. Read on with excitement.

References

Burns, Cynthia Felix. "A Study of the Relationship Between the Use of Planning and Ministry Effectiveness in the Church." Master Thesis. Regent University, 1992.

Benjamin, Dick, Terry Edwards, Jim Durkin, and Dick Iverson. *The Master Builder.* City Christian Publishing, 1985. Boyce, L. F. "Accounting for Churches." *Journal of Accountancy* (February, 1984): 96-102.

Lindgren, Alvin J. *Foundations for Purposeful Church Administration.* New York: Abingdon Press, 1965.

McDonough, Reginald M. "Leading Your Church in Long-Range Planning." Southern Baptist Convention. Sunday School Board. Church Administration Dept., Jean Meritt, Convention Press , 1975.

Van Auken, P. and S. G. Johnson. "Ten Steps to an Effective Evaluation." *Church Administration*, 26 (1984): 28-29.

Chapter 2
Overview of Strategic Planning

But everything should be done in a fitting and orderly way.
—1 Cor, 14:40

In this chapter we present an overview of the strategic planning process. Each of the areas discussed are examined in more detail in later chapters. Our intention here is to provide an introduction to the major components of the process.

What Is Strategic Planning?

The word strategic means "pertaining to strategy." Strategy is derived from the Greek word, strategia, which means generalship, art of the general, or, more broadly, leadership. The word strategic, when used in the context of planning, provides a perspective to planning, which is long run in nature and deals with achieving specified end results. Just as military strategy has as its objective the winning of the war, so, too, strategic planning has as its objective the achievement of ministry goals—the winning of the lost and the equipping of the saints.

Strategic decisions must be differentiated from tactical decisions. The strategic decisions outline the overall game plan or approach, while the tactical decisions involve implementing various activities, which are necessary to carry out a strategy. For example, a church, which decides to change locations because of shifting population trends and industrial development around its present location, is making a strategic decision. Then many other decisions must be made about the exact location, size of the building, parking facilities, etc. These all have long-term implications and are therefore strategic in nature. Other decisions such as wall colors, decor, and air conditioning must then be made. These are tactical decisions needed to carry out or implement the previous strategic decision. Thus, the strategic decision provides the overall framework within which the tactical decisions are made. It is critically important that pastors are able to differentiate between these types of decisions to identify whether the decision has short- or long-term implications.

The Strategic Planning Process

The strategic planning process is basically a matching process involving ministry resources and opportunities. The objective of this process is to peer through the "strategic window" (an opportunity that will not always be there) and identify opportunities which the individual church or ministry is equipped to take advantage of or respond to. Thus the strategic management process can be defined as a managerial process, which involves matching ministry capabilities to ministry opportunities. These opportunities are created over time and decisions revolve around investing or divesting resources to address these opportunities. The context in which these strategic decisions are made is (1) the church or ministry operating environment, (2) ministry purpose or mission, and (3) objectives. This overall process is depicted in Exhibit 2-1. Strategic planning is the process, which ties all these elements together to facilitate strategic choices which are consistent with all three areas and then implements and evaluates these choices. Appendix A presents an outline of a strategic plan.

The successful results of planning described earlier can be achieved through implementing an effective strategic planning process. The following breakdown of this process is a complete outline of the system capable of creating true change in ministry attitudes as well as in productivity. Such a philosophy involves:

1. Defining a ministry purpose and reason for being;

2. Analyzing the environment in which it operates, realistically assessing its strengths and weaknesses, and making assumptions about unpredictable future events;

3. Prescribing written, specific, and measurable objectives in principal result areas contributing to the church or ministry's purpose;

4. Developing strategies on how to use available resources to reach objectives;

5. Developing operational plans to meet objectives including establishing individual objectives and strategies;

6. Evaluating performance to determine whether it is keeping pace with attainment of objectives and is consistent with the defined purpose and changing objectives, strategies, or operational plans in light of the evaluation.

Strategic Planning Process

It is important to recognize at this point what we call "the two Ps." The first P means Product: get the plan in writing. The plan must be something you can hold in your hand, a written product of your efforts. If the plan is not in writing, it is called daydreaming. When it is in writing, you are indicating to yourself and others that you are serious about it. The second P represents Process: every plan must have maximum input from everyone. Those who execute the plan must be involved in construction of the plan. The Bible tells us to obtain input. Note the following three Scripture verses:

> *Without counsel purposes are disappointed: but in the multitude of counselors they are established.—Proverbs 18:22*

Hear counsel, and receive instruction, that thou mayest be wise in thy latter end.—Proverbs 19:20

Every purpose is established by counsel.—Proverbs 20:8

The best way to ensure a plan's failure is to overlook both the product and the process. They are equally important.

While there are many different ways in which a church or ministry could approach the strategic planning process, a systematic approach that carries the organization through a series of integral steps helps to focus attention on a basic set of questions each organization must answer:

1. What will we do? This question focuses attention on the specific needs the church or ministry will try to meet.

2. Who will we do it for? This question addresses the need for a church or ministry to identify the various groups whose needs will be met.

3. How will we do what we want to do? Answering this question forces the organization to think about the many avenues, through which ministry may be channeled.

The strategic planning process used by an organization must force church/ministry leadership to deal with these questions on a continuous basis. The organization evolves over time into what God has established it to be, to do the work that only it can do.

Strategic planning involves the following steps:

1. Defining an organization's purpose and reason for being;

2. Analyzing the environment, assessing its strengths and weaknesses, and making assumptions;

3. Prescribing written, specific, and measurable objectives in the principal result areas that contribute to the organization's purpose;

4. Developing strategies on how to use available resources to meet objectives;

5. Developing operational plans to meet objectives including plans for all individuals in the organization;

6. Setting up control and evaluation procedures to determine if performance is keeping pace with attainment of the objectives and if it is consistent with the defined purpose.

The six steps of the strategic planning process, as illustrated in Exhibit 2-1, are important because they force the organization to consider certain questions. As each step requires the people at various organizational levels to discuss, study, and negotiate the process as a whole , they foster a planning mentality. When the six steps are complete, the end result is a strategic plan for the organization specifying why the organization exists, what it is trying to accomplish, and how resources will be utilized to accomplish objectives and fulfill its purpose.

EXHIBIT 2-1
Strategic Planning Process

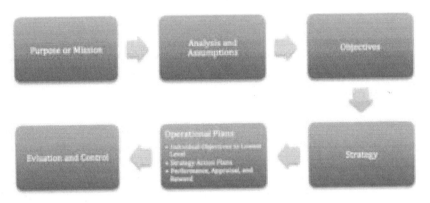

Defining Purpose

The first and probably the most important consideration when developing a strategic plan is to define the purpose, mission, or the "reason for being" of the organization or any specific part of it. This is usually a difficult process even though it may appear simple. For example, a church or ministry, which defines itself as a "group of believers who proclaim the Gospel, may be on the right track but will constantly face the need to explain and expand this definition. Does proclaim mean preach and preach only or does it also include teaching? If teaching is added to the definition, will that involve teaching of spiritual concepts only or would other educational needs be addressed such as preschool, church school, even Bible college or an institution of higher learning? Granted, these things may change as the organization evolves and grows, but thinking through these issues provides a sense of vision and also prevents the church or ministry from engaging in activities which do not fit with what the organization wants to do or be.

Members should try to visualize what they want the organization to become, and should incorporate this dream or vision into their purpose statement. If they can see where they are going and have an image of the real mission of the organization, their plans will fall into place more easily.

The Bible explicitly admonishes us to have a dream and vision. For example, consider the following: Where there is no vision, the people perish (Proverbs 29: 18). Your old men shall dream dreams, your young men shall see visions (Joel 2:28). A vision of what can be accomplished creates the spark and energy for the whole planning and management process. It is important to spend ample time defining this purpose statement. The process should emphasize involving everyone in the dream of how things can be. Without a vision, people just work day-to-day and tend not to be as productive or willing to expend effort.

A good statement of purpose not only clarifies what the church does, it sets boundaries. It defines what the church will not do. It helps limit expectations, and that alone can make it the pastor's best friend (Shelly 1985/86).

Analysis and Assumptions

It is vital for the church to gauge the environment within which it operates. This should be standard practice for all churches. The only way we can manage change is to constantly monitor the environment within which we operate. This analysis stage is where we look at the external environment, internal strengths and weaknesses, and potential threats and opportunities.

For example, many "downtown-churches" have faced a dilemma of whether to remain in the downtown area or move to the suburbs. One church found that its historic location resulted in two significant problems: lack of space to grow and a change in the socioeconomic makeup of the neighborhood. The socioeconomic changes made the church ineffective in meeting the needs of those in the neighborhood who were of different ethnic backgrounds and also made it difficult to attract younger couples into the church.

This church's solution was quite interesting. Members raised funds to buy land and build a new church in a growing part of the community and the conference put a new minister in the old church of the same ethnic background as those in the neighborhood. Everybody won! The old neighborhood church could serve the needs of those who lived there with a great physical plant that included a gym, while the new church was built in an area where there was no church of that denomination and it too grew and prospered.

Many organizations have found it useful to use an analysis framework referred to earlier as a SWOT analysis. SWOT is an acronym for strengths, weaknesses, opportunities, and threats. S t r engths and weaknesses refer to elements internal to the organization, while opportunities and threats are external to the organization. A detailed SWOT analysis helps the church/ministry take a good look at the organization's favorable and unfavorable factors with a view toward building on strengths and eliminating or minimizing weaknesses. At the same time, leadership of a church or ministry must also access external opportunities, which could be pursued, and threats, which must be dealt with in order for the church to survive.

The next stage is to state your major assumptions about spheres over which you have little or absolutely no control, such as the external environment. One good place to start is to extend some of the items studied in the external analysis. Should this stage appear relatively unimportant in developing a strategic plan, consider that by not making explicit assumptions you are making one major implicit assumption—things are going to remain the same and nothing that happens is important enough to affect you!

Establishing Objectives

Often the words "key results," "goals," and "targets" are used synonymously with objectives when thinking about long- and short-term objectives. Think of an archer drawing an arrow and aiming directly at a target. The bull's-eye represents exactly where you want to be at a certain point in time. A pastor wants the whole church aimed at the same target just as an archer wants the arrow aimed at the target. At the other extreme, an archer who shoots arrows off in any direction is liable to hit almost anything, including the wrong target. People get confused and disorganized if they do not know where they are going.

Objectives must be clear, concise, and as written statements, outlining what is to be accomplished in key priority areas over a certain time period, in measurable terms that are consistent with the overall purpose of the organization. Objectives can be classified as routine, problem-solving, innovative, team, personal, or budget performance. Objectives do not determine the future, but they are the means by which the resources and energies are mobilized for the making of the future.

Objectives are the results desired upon completion of the planning period. In the absence of objectives, no sense of direction can be attained in decision-making. In other words, if you don't know where you are going, any road will take you there. In planning, objectives answer one of the basic questions posed in the planning process: Where do we want to go? These objectives become the focal point for strategy decisions.

Another basic purpose served by objectives is in the evaluation of performance. Objectives in the strategic plan become the yard-sticks used for this evaluation. It is impossible to evaluate performance without some standard against which results can be compared. The objectives become the standards for evaluation because they are the statement of results desired by the planner.

Strategy Development

After developing a set of objectives for the time period covered by the strategic plan, a strategy to accomplish those objectives must be formulated. An overall strategy must first be designed; then the operational strategies must be developed.

Strategy alternatives are the alternate courses of action evaluated by management before commitment is made to a specific option outlined in the strategic plan. Thus, strategy is the link between objectives and results.

Operational Plans

After all the steps have been taken and a strategy has been developed to meet your objectives and goals, it is time to develop an operational or action plan. The operational plan stage is the "action" or "doing" stage. Here you hire, fire, build, advertise, and so on. How many times has a group of people planned something, gotten enthusiastic, and then nothing happened? This is usually because they did not complete an operational or action plan to implement their strategy.

Operational plans must be developed for all the areas that are used to support the overall strategy. These include production, communication, finance, and staffing. Each of these more detailed plans is designed to spell out what needs to happen in a given area to implement the strategic plan.

Supporting the operational plans are the individual plans of all members of the organization. These are shown as steps SA, SB, and SC in Exhibit 2-1. When planning is carried from the top to the lowest level in the organization, everyone becomes involved in setting and negotiating personal objectives, which support the organization's objectives. Then each person begins to develop an individual action plan, which is used to accomplish these personal objectives. Finally, the personal performance appraisal, which must be done on an individual basis, uses those individual objectives as the basis of appraisal and reward.

Evaluation and Control

Failure to establish procedures to appraise and control the strategic plan can lead to less than optimal performance. A plan is not complete until the controls are identified, and the procedures for recording and transmitting control information to the administrators of the plan are established. Many organizations fail to understand the importance of establishing procedures to appraise and control the planning process. Control should be a natural follow-through in developing a plan.

Planning and control should be integral processes. The strategic planning process results in a strategic plan. This plan is implemented (activities are performed in the manner described in the plan) and results are produced. These results are attendance, baptisms, contributions, and accompanying constituent attitudes, behaviors, etc. Information on these and other key result areas is given to administrators, who compare the results with objectives to evaluate performance. This performance evaluation identifies the areas where decisions must be made to adjust activities, people, or finances. The actual decision-making controls the plan by altering it to accomplish stated objectives, and a new cycle begins.

Individual performance appraisal is a vital part of this step. Rewards or reprimands must be related to the personal achievement or lack of achievement of agreed-upon objectives. This creates a work environment where people know what to do and rewards are tied to performance.

Strategic Planning as a Process

The word process refers to a series of actions directed to an end. The actions are the activities in which the church or ministry engages to accomplish objectives and fulfill its mission. There are several important reasons for viewing strategic planning as a process. First, a change in any component of the process will affect most or all of the other components. For example, a change in purpose or objective will lead to new analysis, strategies, and evaluations. Thus, major changes, which affect the organization, must lead to a reevaluation of all the elements of the plan.

A second reason for viewing strategic planning as a process is that a process can be studied and improved. A church or ministry just getting involved in strategic planning will need to review the whole process, on an annual basis not only to account for changing environmental forces but to improve or refine the plan. Purpose statements, objectives, strategies, and appraisal techniques can be fine tuned over time as the planners gain more experience and as new and better information becomes available.

Finally and perhaps most importantly, involvement in the strategic planning process can become the vehicle through which the whole organization mobilizes its energies to accomplish its purpose. If all members of the organization can participate in the process in some way, an atmosphere can be created within the organization that implies that doing the right things and doing things right is everybody's job. Participation instills ownership. It's not "my plan" or "their plan" but "God's plan" that becomes important; and everyone will want to make a contribution to make it happen.

Strategy Implementation

The focus of this book is on the strategic planning process, which results in the development of a strategic plan. This plan becomes the blueprint for carrying out the many activities in which a church or ministry is involved. There are many other issues that determine the effectiveness of an organization which are beyond the scope of this book. These issues essentially revolve around implementing the strategic plan through (1) staffing and training personnel and volunteers (2) developing organization relationships among staff/volunteers (3) achieving commitment, (4) developing a positive organizational culture, (5) leadership styles, and (6) personnel evaluation and reward systems.

Our lack of discussion of these topics is due to space limitation and a desire to keep the length of the book manageable for readers. While the scriptures state that "where there is no vision, the people perish" (KJV, Proverbs 29:8), it is also true that without people, especially the right people, the vision will perish. Both effective planning and implementation are needed to create an effective organization. The strategic plan concentrates on "doing the right things" while implementation concentrates on "doing things right." An example of an entire strategic plan for a ministry is presented in Appendix C.

Summary

In this chapter we have presented an overview of the strategic planning process in which a series of thought-provoking questions must be answered. The process is a set of integral steps which carries the planners through a sequence that involves providing answers to these questions and then continually rethinking and reevaluating these answers as the organization and its environment change.

A helpful tool at this stage is the Planning and Management Systems Audit form provided in Appendix D. This form, when thoughtfully filled out, will provide an assessment of your current position in terms of planning and management of your organization. It will help point out where to direct your efforts to improve the efficiency and effectiveness of the organization God has entrusted to your leadership.

Planning Process Worksheet

This worksheet is provided to aid your church or ministry in starting the strategic planning projects.

1. Who should be involved in the planning process?

   _____

   _____

   _____

2. Where will planning sessions be held?

   _____

   _____

   _____

3. When will planning sessions be held?

   _____

   _____

   _____

4. What types of background material do participants need prior to starting the first session?

_____
_____
_____

5. Who will lead the process? Who will ultimately be responsible for arranging sessions, getting material typed, reproduced, and distributed?

6.

_____
_____
_____

7. When and how will members of the staff, board, congregation, or others be involved in the process?

_____
_____
_____

8. How will the results be communicated to everyone in the organization?

_____
_____
_____

9. Who will train/supervise staff members in working with their own staff and volunteers in setting objectives, developing action plans, and performance appraisals?

_____
_____
_____

10. How frequently will the process be reviewed and by whom?

_____
_____
_____

11. Who will be responsible for dealing with external groups (Bishops, media people, consultants) in preparing the plan?

_____
_____
_____

References

Engstrom, Ted W. and Edward R. Dayton. *Defining the Mission. World Vision*, 1984.
Shelly, Judith Allen. *Not Just a Job: Serving Christ in Your Work*. Downers Grove, Ill.:
    InterVarsity Press, 1985.

Chapter 3
Defining Your Purpose

Where there is no vision, the people perish. (KJV)
—*Proverbs 29:8*

This chapter outlines the first step in the strategic planning process. Without a clear and carefully considered statement of purpose all other stages of the process will be misguided. We will therefore discuss the value of defining the ministry's purpose, describe how to write effective statements of purpose or mission, and present two examples of mission statements.

The Importance of Defining Purpose

The first and probably most important consideration when developing a strategic plan is to define the purpose, mission, or "reason for being" for the organization or any specific part of it. This is usually a difficult process. Peter Drucker, a management consultant and writer, has led the way in stressing the importance of defining purpose. An organization develops to satisfy a need in the marketplace. Drucker states that the organization's purpose is defined by the want the customer satisfies by buying a product or service. Thus, satisfying the customer is the mission and purpose of every business (1974, 79). Organizations need a clear definition of purpose and mission. This raises the questions: "What is our purpose?" and "What should it be?" Drucker's answer is that only a clear definition of the mission and purpose of the business makes possible clear and realistic business objectives. It is the foundation for priorities, strategies, plans, and work assignments. It is the starting point for the design of managerial structure and jobs (1974, 75).

Clearly, if purpose is defined casually or introspectively, or if the list of key result areas neglects some of the less obvious threats and opportunities, the organization is at risk. As Calvin Coolidge put it: "No enterprise can exist for itself alone. It ministers to some great need, it performs some great service not for itself but for others; or failing therein it ceases to be profitable and ceases to exist."

It is in this purpose statement that the vision and the dream for the church or ministry must be reflected. This purpose statement sets the stage for all planning. Objectives, which are covered later in the text, must by their very nature contribute to achieving what is in the purpose statement. In a study of private Christian college and university administrations, it was discovered that all those surveyed had a purpose and mission statement, but only 50 percent had specific measurable objectives of what was to be accomplished.

A mission statement aids a church or ministry by:

1. Giving it a reason for being, and an explanation to members and others as to why it exists as an organization;

2. Helping to place boundaries around the ministry and thus defining what it will and will not do;

3. Describing the need the organization is attempting to meet in the world;

4. Giving a general description of how the organization is going to respond to that need;.

5. Acting as the hook on which the primary objectives of the organization can be hung;

6. Helping to form the basis for the ethos (or culture) of the organization;

7. Helping to communicate to those outside what the organization is all about ("Defining the Mission" 1984, 1, 2).

Writing a Statement of Purpose

The following list (Lambert 1975, 28) provides several helpful tips on writing and evaluating a purpose statement.

1. Identify the mission of that part of the organization to which the group is accountable. A parish council may be accountable to the parish at large, the pastor, bishop, diocesan pastoral council, or all of these. The liturgy committee will be accountable to the parish council. The director of religious education may be accountable to the religious education committee, pastor, or both.

2. Determine that portion of the above mission statement for which the group is responsible. While the parish council is accountable for the total parish operation, the maintenance committee, for example, will be responsible only for that portion of the parish council's mission that deals with maintaining the grounds and buildings in a usable and functional state.

3. Prepare a rough draft of the mission statement, which covers the purpose of the group and the major activities it performs. With a working team, such as a parish staff or parish council, a rough draft mission statement can be developed at an all-day meeting, using an outside facilitator who is familiar with communications techniques, group processes, and the concept of mission statements. The meeting can begin with each individual writing

a version of the mission statement on newsprint. When these drafts are all assembled, the group can review each one for clarity and understanding. Finally, consolidate those portions that are similar so that only areas of wide disagreement are left. At this point, negotiations can be carried out between members of the group until there is general agreement on all points. The final result is the rough draft of the mission statement.

A purpose statement must be built around several points:

1. Congregational Care: typically this includes corporate worship, administration of the sacraments, pastoral care, fellowship, and the nurturing, education, and training for Christian discipleship of the members.

2. Outreach and Evangelism: this part of the statement focuses on the imperative to go out and confront individuals outside the church with the good news that Jesus Christ is their Redeemer and Savior. While the first part of this outline was directed toward the parish's ministry to persons inside the gathered community, this part emphasizes the parish's responsibility to individuals outside the church.

3. Witness and Mission: the emphasis here is on the church's responsibility to be a living witness for Christ to the groups, organizations, structures, and institutions outside the church in the world. This also helps the members to understand both the legitimacy and the imperative for the parish's involvement in the social, economic, and political issues in the local community. (Schaller 1965, 33)

Sample Mission Statements

It might be helpful at this point to examine a mission statement prepared by a church and a ministry. Note that these statements reflect the uniqueness of the organizations in terms of their reason for being and also serve as guidelines for what the organization should be doing. These statements were developed through a process involving many people and over a period of six to eight months. Initial statements were revised many times to add specificity and clarity to the terms used to define purpose.

Mission Statement
Monroe Covenant Church
Monroe, Louisiana

Statement of Purpose

Monroe Covenant Church is a full-gospel (charismatic), interdenominational congregation deeply rooted in the historic evangelical faith. Our basic purpose is to (1) glorify and please God, (2) edify and train believers, and (3) evangelize and saturate the world with the Gospel of Jesus Christ. Our emphasis is on the three "B's: Believing, Becoming, and Belonging."

Believing

We are a church that believes that our duty is to:

1. Bring people to a saving knowledge of Jesus Christ as the only way to salvation;

2. Help people experience the Baptism in the Holy Spirit with all His gifts and fruits; Train Christians to share their faith with others and to proclaim the Gospel;

3. Do the compassionate and powerful works of Christ in the world;

4. Give practical application to our Christian faith in the areas of (1) family life, (2) church life, (3) job, (4) ethics, (5) morality, (6) personal relationships, (7) financial integrity, (8) civic responsibility, and (9) community involvement;

5. Seek ways to build the unity of the Church by recognizing and relating with individuals and Churches outside our local congregation and, in so doing, identify with and incorporate into the larger Church in our city, state, and the Church Universal.

Becoming

We are a church that desires to:

1. Increase in the knowledge and power of (1) God's Word, (2) prayer, and (3) fellowship with believers, according to Acts 2:42;

2. Grow in our ability to worship God personally and corporately;

3. Grow in our commitment to the Lord as expressed in our loyalty, faithfulness, obedience, integrity, and love;

4. Grow in individual and corporate freedom in Christ by using all the means of grace, among which are healing, counseling, deliverance, and forgiveness, to be Christians who then might be able to help others also enter that same freedom in Christ;

5. Increase in making a difference for the Kingdom of God in our society.

Belonging

We are a church that emphasizes belonging by:

1. Committing to work out practical Christian relationships according to the "one another" passages of the New Testament and, in so doing to the best of our understanding, fulfill what the Bible describes as covenant love and covenant relationship;

2. Teaching, identifying, training, recognizing, and releasing the many diverse gifts in the Body of Christ so that believers better find and function in their God-given places;

3. Calling for the many diverse needs of the individual members of the church;

4. Attitudes and actions of friendliness and acceptance so that everyone will know that we care for them.

Mission Statement
Beeson Center for Biblical Preaching and Pastoral Leadership
Asbury Theological Seminary
Wilmore, Kentucky

Our Mission

The Beeson Center for Biblical Preaching and Pastoral Leadership exists to serve the church through serving pastors. Our purpose is the advanced training of pastors in preaching and leadership skills for the sake of Christ, to increase the effectiveness of their ministry, and to equip God's people under the authority of scripture and in obedience to the call for scriptural holiness and love.

Our Message

The Beeson Center for Biblical Preaching and Pastoral Leadership is committed to the following expression of this purpose.

1. Faithful proclamation of the Word of God is the foundation of ministry. Faithful proclamation begins with faithful pastors who experience and understand the truth of God's word in their own lives. Effective preaching requires rightly interest setting scripture. Effective communication implies not only speaking the truth, but also speaking in terms which can be understood and appropriated by the culture in which we live. The Beeson Center exists to train pastors to better understand and communicate the gospel as teachers, preachers, and models of the Word of God.

2. Worship forms and energizes the community of God. The Word proclaimed by the preacher does not exist in isolation, but in the totality of worship, which communicates the gospel on many levels. The Beeson Center exists to foster the creative integration of proclamation into overall worship in terms which honor God and speak to our times.

3.   Every church, informed by Biblical mandates such as the Great Commission, must form its own vision. Each pastor should articulate a personal vision and call. Pastors and churches have individual gifts that function best when applied to appropriate missions. The Beeson Center exists to foster the pastor's understanding of his or her own gifts and call, and to develop a vision for the church they serve.

4.   The church today exists in a world, which is defined and formed by the growing power of media and technology. Each generation throughout church history has learned to use the technological tools of its day in the service of Christ. The Beeson Center is committed to the integration of excellent media and computer technology in the communication of the gospel of Christ.

5.   The ministry of the church consists of the work of all Christians as they are faithful to Christ. The pastor is called to equip and train the whole people of God for this ministry. The Beeson Center exists to provide training and guidance for pastors in the development of staff and lay ministry.

Our Market

1.   The Beeson Center for Biblical Preaching and Pastoral Leadership at Asbury Theological Seminary begins with its base in the Wesleyan-Holiness and Methodist traditions of Christianity. We seek first to reach and to serve pastors in this tradition from the historic perspective of the seminary.

2.   We seek to be inclusive, serving both those women and men from all races who form our historic constituencies, and also pastors and churches from other theological traditions. We seek to focus our service for young pastors of promise primarily through a year-long program in Biblical preaching and pastoral leadership. We seek to focus our service to established pastors primarily through short-term, intensive programs in specific aspects of teaching and leadership.

3.   We seek to serve the church-at-large through research, publications, and media instruction.

Our Measures for Our Future

4.   The Beeson Center will incorporate through the existing Doctor of Ministry program a one-year; on-site DMin program in Biblical Preaching and Leadership which will be funded by the Beeson Scholars Program

and housed in the Beeson Center. We seek, by 1993, to have 12 scholars on campus, and 24 by1995. This program will concentrate on pastors early in their career who show unusual promise as preachers and leaders for the future of the church.

5. The Beeson Center will establish the Senior Pastor Program of short-term study opportunities for established pastors. The program will offer intensive study and training opportunities in preaching, theological and spiritual formation, leadership, church administration, and programming for active senior pastors. We would like to have 40 pastors involved by 1993 and 80 by 1995.

6. The Beeson Center will establish a research and publicity program beginning with a journal or newsletter on preaching and leadership in 1992.

7. The Beeson Center is committed to the use of advanced technology and media resources in teaching and for the use of the church. The Beeson Center will develop a system of optic fiber communication within the Asbury Theological Seminary campus to promote the use of media and technology for teaching in classroom settings. The Center will also promote the development of video instructional resources for pastors and churches, concentrating on preaching, worship, church programs, and related issues. The Center will develop the ability to offer teaching programs to pastors and churches through satellite relay for instruction away from the Wilmore campus.

8. The Beeson Center will sponsor and lead a program of computer communications, offering the library and media resources of Asbury Seminary to pastors through computer link-up. This will be in cooperation with the existing program of the library, expanding as resources and technology allow to make more and more of our resources accessible by computer link-up.

9. The Beeson Center will seek to network with pastors in order to identify pastoral needs to be addressed in the program to provide resources to pastors, to identify potential participants in the various programs, and to provide ongoing opportunities for ministry for them.

10. The Beeson Center, in cooperation with the Pastoral Care Division of the Seminary, will sponsor the development of an Assessment Center for pastors and students. This center will offer personal testing and evaluation

in order to help students understand their own gifts, values, and resources and develop personal vision and goals to guide them in their ministry.

Our Spirit

The Beeson Center for Biblical Preaching and Pastoral Leadership seeks to serve pastors and the church. We seek to form bridges between the academic world and the pastor, between the seminary and the church, and between the gospel proclaimed and a culture in need of Christ.

The Center will be a focus for learning and personal growth. Excellence in ministry involves using the right tools for the right purpose. But ministry begins with individuals, who have surrendered their lives to service in the name of Christ. The church needs the Spirit of God unleashed through committed individuals who combine wisdom and skill in the execution of their ministry. We will seek to foster a marriage of mind and Spirit in the context of preaching and ministry.

We will not be a place where stock formulas are given. We will seek to grow a community where people bring practical needs and find wisdom, encouragement, and challenge.

We will listen to the world respectfully and carefully. But, modem American culture will not ask all our questions, nor supply all the answers. We will seek to be a community that listens most attentively to God and God's word, and to respond in obedience.

Evaluating A Purpose Statement

The list below can be used as a guide to evaluate a statement of purpose. The goal is to devise a statement that really represents what the organization wants to be or should be to survive.

1. Broadness of scope and continuity of application: The statement should be broad enough to cover all significant areas of activity expected of the organization without a specific termination period indicated.

2. Functional commitment: The nature of the works, tasks, or activities to be performed must be defined in terms that will determine clearly the validity of the group or organization.

3. Resource commitment: The statement should include a commitment to cost-effective utilization of available resources.

4. Unique or distinctive nature of work: Every unit in an organization should make some unique or at least distinctive contribution. If there are two or more peer units in an organization with identical mission statements, the risk of duplicated effort is obvious.

5. Description of services to be offered.

6. Description of group or groups to be served.

7. Geographical area to be covered.

Sometimes it is useful to use a series of questions to evaluate a purpose statement after it is written. A "no" answer to one of the questions means the statement needs to be reworded to more clearly reflect the organization's basic reason for being. The following lists of questions may be useful.

1. Does it contain all important commitments?

2. Does it clearly state the function?

3. Is there a clear determination of relationships to the rest of the organization?

4. Is it distinct from the mission statements of other groups in the organization?

5. Is it short, to the point, and understandable?

6. Is it continuing in nature?

7. Does it state to whom the group is accountable?

Generally a purpose statement can reflect whether the church wants to be local, regional, national, or international, the needs to be met, and so forth. The word "service" is often included in the mission statement of any organization.

The purpose statement needs to answer the question of why your church or ministry is needed in the first place. Plenty of other organizations exist. Discuss and know specifically what need you are meeting. For example, Victory Christian Center in Tulsa determined it was a local church with an international outreach. Morris Cerullo World Evangelism, based in San Diego, is truly an international ministry. Victory Christian Center and World Evangelism are quite different, but their primary reason for being is the same.

In an established denominational church, the focal purpose statement must reflect the support of the overall church statement of purpose. For example, a local Methodist church purpose statement should reflect the overall beliefs and doctrine of the United Methodist Church. John Wesley's own statement of the purpose of a Methodist Society is described in The Nature, Design, and General Rules of the United Societies (1743):

> *A company united in order to pray together, to receive the word of exhortation, and to watch over one another in love, that they may help each other to work out their salvation.*

Denominational organizations thus must make sure their purpose is aligned with the overall denomination's purpose. For example, when the pastor of one city's First United Methodist Church led his staff through this planning process, they all had to be constantly aware of the basic Methodist beliefs to be sure the purpose statement reflected those beliefs. This does not mean that the First United Methodist Church does not have the freedom of an unaligned or nondenominational church to have a vision and dream. It just means that the church had to be conscious of its roots to remain consistent.

Summary

By verbalizing and putting in writing the vision God has given you for your church or ministry, you, in effect, state the unique reason God has brought your organization into existence. This provides the sense of direction and focus for what you do. What you do must be a function of who you are. The statement of purpose translates what God has divinely ordained into a mission for your church or ministry to fulfill.

Purpose Statement Worksheet

This worksheet is provided to aid your church or ministry in starting the strategic, planning process.

1. Write a statement for the following areas: Congregational care statement:

    _____

    _____

    _____

2. Outreach and evangelism statement:

    _____

    _____

    _____

3. Witness and mission work statement:

    _____

    _____

    _____

    Now evaluate the statement using the list of questions provided earlier.

    Next submit it to others familiar with your organization to evaluate your statement of purpose and offer suggestions on improving the statement. In other words, does the statement say to others what you want it to say?

References

Drucker, Peter F. *Management: Tasks, Responsibilities, Practices.* New York: Harper & Row, 1974.

Lambert, Norman M. *Managing Church Groups.* Dayton, Ohio: Pflaum Pub., 1975.

Schaller, Lyle. *Planning for Protestantism in Urban America.* New York: Abingdon Press, 1965.

Chapter 4
Analysis and Assumptions

> *It is the glory of God to conceal a matter; to search out a matter is the glory of kings.*
> *—Proverbs 25:2*

External Analysis

It is vital for a church or ministry to gauge the environment within which it operates. This should be standard practice for all organizations. It is important to realize that anything that can happen probably will, and that there is no truly accurate way to predict what the future will bring. The only way we can manage change is to constantly monitor the environment within which we operate. Examples for business might be the trends we see in gross national product, governmental control regulation, the labor movement, interest rates, consumer preference; industry surveys, marketing research, Dow Jones stock averages, recent commodity prices, and so forth.

This environmental analysis stage is where we look at the past, identify trends, and in effect, take the pulse of the environment in which the organization operates. Environmental analysis should not be confused with an assumption.

As an example, an environmental analysis for a television ministry might include the following elements: ("Cable Connections for Christ" 1985)

- In August 1984, cable penetration was estimated at 42.9 percent of American television households by the Nielsen service, with 36.1 million of the 83.3 million homes with television having cable. Arbitron's estimates show U.S. Cable penetration to stand at 41 percent, or 34.5 million households.

- Pat Robertson, president of Christian Broadcasting Network (CBN), has stated that 11 million subscribers who have access to CBN are watching it in a given week.

- Research by the American Resource Bureau indicates that the total audience for religious programs is about ten million people, or roughly 10 percent of the adult viewing public.

- There are currently more than. 60 syndicated religious programs broadcast, and dozens more that do not qualify for syndicated status and measurement.

- Twenty-four-hour Christian satellite networks deliver programming to cable stations across the United States.

- Like so much of its work, the church may be learning that cable television must be a local ministry if it is to be evangelistically effective.

- Most of the mass media ministries are used for education and growth, reaching the already churched. But in local neighborhoods, cable television has proven to be an effective witness for converting the unsaved to Christ.

- Cable television is one of the best methods of extending the walls of the church and enlarging the outreach of its ministry into the local community.

- Television can be a tremendous public relations tool. Many churches today never have any influence in their community. Many are nonexistent as far as their community is concerned. They have no voice, influence, or even contact with those outside their fellowship.

- Ministry via cable television—when, it is coupled with local church—provides a nonthreatening medium through which viewers can participate.

Assessing Opportunities and Threats

Opportunities and threats related to the external environment are analyzed to determine if any action (strategy) is needed to deal with them. For example a large number of homeless people in a downtown area close to a church could provide an opportunity for ministry aimed at this group, and for a specific outreach program for this group. Alternatively, the church may decide that even though the opportunity exists, they do not have the resources to begin ministry. Opportunities cannot be pursued if they are not recognized and analyzed.

The same is true for threats. A ministry that is not well financed and in heavy debt may risk losing a key leader due to death or illness or the "halo" effect of bad publicity of other ministries as a threat to the existence or at least the effectiveness of the ministry. Recognizing threats and analyzing the possible ramifications of events helps avoid many crises by developing contingency plans for dealing with such situations. Some have referred to this as "what if" and "what then" analysis. In other words, asking the questions "What if this happens?" and then "What do we do if this happens?" helps a church or ministry deal with major events which might be detrimental to the organization.

External analysis should evaluate at least seven factors (Migliore, 1988, 74):

1. Economic trends in the locality, the geographic region, and the nation. Examples of these trends are changes in personal income, employment, land values, and industry location.

2. Demographic trends including shifts in age groups, education levels, numbers of widows and retired people, and shifts of population to different geographic areas.

3. Community issues of urban versus suburban development, growth or decline of commercial activities and transportation facilities.

4. Changes in the services offered to people in the community. Who is offering the services? Are services primarily shifting into governmental hands or private sponsorship? How effective are these services in meeting the needs of the community?

5. Trends in competition for prime-time Sunday mornings and evenings and perhaps weekday evenings. What other things are going on that present competition for that time?

6. Church attendance trends in the community and region and reasons for changes in these trends. What activities in churches are proving to be the most popular at this time?

7. Changes in social values. What do people in the community view as important? Is churchgoing an important value? Evaluation in this area can involve issues such as the strength of family relationships, attitudes toward moral values, and so forth.

This stage in the planning process does not merely involve gathering data, getting it on paper, and forgetting about it. The environment must be constantly monitored.

Internal Analysis

At the organization level, another step in a thorough analysis is a full audit of the organization. A complete study of the church's emphasis on its ministries, management, policies, and procedures is needed. Also included in this environmental analysis is a study of the management system. A management questionnaire gives management information on the effectiveness of the management system and brings major problems to the surface. A method for auditing the planning system is needed. One way of doing this is through a questionnaire reviewing the planning environment, organizational structure, management philosophy and style, planning process, and other factors relating to the organization. The result is a thorough understanding of the planning system.

The data collected in the audit can then be analyzed to determine strengths and weaknesses in the planning system. The most important are then included in the strengths-and-weaknesses part of the planning process.

It is useful to build a data base. The congregation or partner base should be one element studied. The more you know about the people being served, the better you can meet their needs. Many successful businesses, such as Wal-Mart, are continually doing research to learn more about their customers. A ministry should do the same thing. Information can be gathered on such factors as family size, marital status, age levels, where people work, people's needs, how long members have been in the congregation, whether people own or rent, and where they live. All of these are good questions to ask. For example, Victory Christian Center developed a profile of its congregation using modem marketing research techniques and found that 53 percent are under age 35, 48 percent have been attending Victory one year or less, 52 percent live within five miles of the church, 31 percent are single, 8 percent are single parents, and so forth.

Several examples of questionnaires which could be modified for use in conducting an analysis of constituents are presented in Appendix E.

The Church and Community Survey Workbook, published by the Southern Baptist Convention Press, Nashville, Tennessee, does a good job of describing how to conduct meaningful surveys. The book contains sample questions and many fine ideas. It is a must for anyone involved in serious church or ministry planning.

Assessing Strengths and Weaknesses

After you have identified the purpose and considered the environment in which you operate, it is important to objectively assess the strengths and weaknesses of your church or ministry. In doing this, planners can learn from athletic coaches. They are constantly assessing the strengths and weaknesses of their team and the opponent. They try to maximize their strengths on game day and improve on their weaknesses during practice.

Organizations have certain strengths which make them uniquely suited to carry out their tasks. Conversely, they have certain weaknesses which inhibit their abilities to fulfill their purposes. Like athletic coaches, managers who hope to accomplish their tasks need to carefully evaluate the strengths and weaknesses of the organization.

Among the things to evaluate are human, financial, facilities, equipment, and natural resources (Migliore 1988, 83-85):

1. Financial resources of the church including operating funds, special funds, income, and expenditures

    What has been our performance over the last five years in adhering to budget limits?

    What is our ability to raise funds when needed?

2. Equipment and space

    Is it adequate for present needs and for planning future needs?

    Is it in good operating condition?

    Is it costly to maintain or operate?

3. The demographics of the congregation

    How many people do we have in each age group?

What are the basic categories of jobs and income levels?

What percentage of the congregation consists of retired people or widows?

4. Sociological profile of the church

   Are we conservative or liberal?

   Are we community minded?

   Does our church collaborate with other community agencies and institutions?

   As a church, what are our primary interests and social values?

5. Power structure of the church

   Who makes the decisions and by what process?

6. Church organization and management

   Quality of staffing, lay leadership, personnel policies, financial and business management capabilities, organizational structure.

7. Present programs

   What are they?

   Is the leadership in each program effective?

   How much interest and support from the congregation does each program have?

It is fairly easy to identify the strengths in each of these areas. When you attempt to define weaknesses, it becomes a little more painful. Often, organizations must engage outside consultants to be able to candidly pinpoint their limitations. But weaknesses and limitations must be recognized before you move on. All the evaluations listed in the environmental analysis can be separated into strengths and weaknesses.

Often church planning groups identify strengths first and write them on a blackboard. Through discussions, the group agrees on perhaps five major strengths. Then each person writes two or three weaknesses of the organization down on paper, which are copied onto the board to generate discussion. Only with a candid appraisal of strengths and weaknesses can realistic objectives be set.

Making Assumptions

The next step is to make your major assumptions about spheres over which you have little or absolutely no control (e.g., the external environment). One good place to start is to extend some of the items studied in the external analysis.

Assumptions inherent in the field of church or ministry management might well include such statements as those listed below:

1. Television and radio programming costs will continue to skyrocket, especially during prime time.

2. Church-related capital will remain tax exempt, and contributions to church and ministry organizations will continue to be tax deductible.

3. Nursery care during the Sunday morning service will remain a priority item sought after by mothers of infants.

4. Providing a family service during the week will continue to (a) enhance church unity and (b) be an effective means to teach members on such issues as proper tithing practice.

A common thread is noted in church ministries that are growing and thriving under their founders. In such organizations, plans have the basic assumption that these people remain in good health and continue as senior pastors. These founding pastors are important to the continued success of their ministries.

A list of certain assumptions that characterize the church/ministry should be developed. Assumptions are those thoughts and ideas that we take for granted about ourselves, God, and others. These assumptions are basic beginning points in the church's care, interest, and concern for people.

Below are some assumptions that fit the strategic planning model.

1. Quality leads to quantity. The quality of faith leads to greatness of faith. The quality of care for people leads to more people.

2. A commitment to excellence produces confidence in ministry and care. If I am committed to excellence in my personal life spiritually, emotionally, educationally, professionally, and socially, then people will have confidence in my interest in and care of them.

3. The Holy Spirit, along with the church, is able, willing, and free to break in and carry on His work in non-spectacular, non-manipulative, and surprising ways.

4. Each church is a new creation and should have differing forms of style and practices suited to that particular group.

5. You cannot manufacture the Holy Spirit's genuine working. You can only be in a position to see and enjoy it when it happens.

Assumptions must be directly related to action. Note the relationship between assumption and proposed action in the following example.

Assumption: Assume that a battleship fleet port will be located in the Lake Charles, Louisiana, area.

The plan for a church in the Lake Charles, Louisiana area is based in part on the external analysis that has thoroughly looked at what is going on in that area. In this case, you see that there is a chance for real economic change, new prosperity, people moving in, and so forth. Then you base your plan on an assumption. You either assume the port is in your area or you do not. How does this translate into action?

Action: Negotiate a land option.

That overgrown lot next to the church that has been an eyesore for years will go up in value in a hurry if the port is located in the area. Now is the time to negotiate an option to buy to cover a two-year period, not in five years when the need is great and the price is sky-high. The planner should also protect the church if the naval base goes somewhere else. With declining industry in the area, it is possible land values could go down.

The key is knowing what is going on and being alert to opportunities. Then develop a full plan based on a few assumptions. If an assumption changes, the plan changes.

The outline in Appendix B is a useful tool for internal and external analysis. Answering all the questions can be a good start in assessing the organization in several areas.

Summary

This chapter emphasized the importance of coming to grips with the external and internal environments in which you must work to fulfill your mission. Minimizing weaknesses and capitalizing on strengths helps bolster the ability of an organization to operate in its external environment. Specifying the assumptions provides a basis for thoughtful consideration of the basic premises on which you operate. They should also cause you to ponder the "What if," "What then" scenarios that help avoid disruptions in the organization's operations through contingency planning.

Analysis and Assumptions Worksheet

This worksheet will aid you in applying the concepts discussed in this chapter to your church or ministry.

1. List key environmental factors for your plan.

    NATIONAL

    REGIONAL

    LOCAL

2. List the assumptions on which your plan is based.

References

Joffe, Bruce. "Cable Connections for Christ." *Charisma*, 10(72) (1985): 74-78, 80.

Migliore, R. Henry. *The Use of Strategic Planning for Churches and Ministries*. Tulsa, OK.: Harrison House, 1988.

Chapter 5
Establishing Objectives

*I press on toward the goal to win the prize for which God has
called me heavenward in Christ Jesus.*
—Phil. 3:14

In this chapter we discuss establishing objectives, the third step in the strategic
planning process. After the purpose or mission of the church or ministry has been
defined, internal and external analysis completed, and assumptions made, then—
and only then—can objectives be considered.

One writer has said, "You cannot achieve goals if you do not have any."
Sometimes this idea is so simple that many people overlook it. In order to
accomplish anything, we have to first purpose in our hearts to do it. We have
to make up our minds. If we do not, we just waste our time and energy and find
ourselves going around in circles, looking back at the past and wondering where
it went.

Nature and Role of Objectives

The words key results, goals, and targets are often used synonymously when
talking about long- and short-term objectives. Whatever the term used, the idea
is to focus on a specific set of target activities and outcomes to be accomplished.
Think of the analogy of the archer used earlier. A pastor wants his whole church
aimed at the same target just as an archer wants his arrow aimed at the bull's-eye.
People get confused and disorganized if they do not know where they are going.
The success or failure of a nonprofit organization is based on its ability to set
goals, as well as on tools with which to measure progress.

There are at least six reasons why nonprofit organizations (such as churches
and ministries) fail to set clear-cut objectives.

1. Many nonprofit managers fear accountability.

2. Many projects continue even when they no longer serve an organization's
   goals.

3. Nonprofits normally undertake any activity for which money is available.

4. Some nonprofit managers fear hard-nosed evaluation may undermine
   humanitarian instincts.

5. Nonprofit managers must spend a great deal of time on activities that do not
   further their goals (meeting with donors, fund raising, explaining programs,
   and so forth).

6.   Nonprofits have no financial report cards to tell them how they are doing.

As objectives are established in the organization, some of these reasons may not be applicable. However, most of this list could be applied in any type of organizational setting.

Objectives are clear, concise written statements outlining what is to be accomplished in key areas in a certain time period, in objectively measurable terms. Objectives can be classified as routine, problem solving, innovative, team, personal, and budget performance. Drucker states that "objectives are not fate; they are direction. They are not commands, but they are commitments. They do not determine the future, but they are the means by which the resources and energies of the operation can be mobilized for the making of the future" (1954, 102).

Objectives can be set at upper organizational levels in areas such as growth, finances, physical resources, staff development and attitudes. They are also needed in sub-units, departments, or divisions of an organization. Most important, all organizational objectives must be consistent. Thus, a department's objectives should lead to accomplishing the overall organization's goals.

Objectives serve two fundamental purposes. First, they serve as a road map. Objectives are the results desired upon completion of the planning period. In the absence of objectives, no sense of direction can be attained in decision making. In planning, objectives answer one of the basic questions posed in the planning process: Where do we want to go? These objectives become the focal point for strategy decisions.

Another basic purpose served by objectives is in the evaluation of performance. The objectives in the strategic plan become the yardsticks used to evaluate performance. It is impossible to evaluate performance without some standard with which results can be compared. The objectives become the standards for evaluating performance because they are the statement of results desired by the planner.

Objectives are often considered the neglected area of management because in many situations there is a failure to set objectives, or the objectives which are set forth are unsound and therefore lose much of their effectiveness. In fact, a fairly recent approach to management, called management by objectives (MBO), has emphasized the need for setting objectives as a basic managerial process.

Alternatives to Managing by Objectives

One way to be convinced of the usefulness and power of managing by objectives is to consider some of the alternatives. (Thompson and Strickland 1986,52)

1.   *Managing By Extrapolation (MBE)*. This approach relies on the principle "If it ain't broke, don't fix it." The basic idea is to keep on doing about the

same things in about the same ways because what you are doing (1) works well enough and (2) has gotten you this far. The basic assumption is that, for whatever reason, "your act is together," so why worry?; the future will take care of itself and things will work out all right.

2. *Managing By Crisis (MBC).* This approach to administration is based upon the concept that the strength of any really good manager is solving problems. Since there are plenty of crises around—enough to keep everyone occupied—managers ought to focus their time and energy on solving the most pressing problems of today. MBC is, essentially, reactive rather than proactive, and the events that occur dictate management decisions.

3. *Managing By Subjectives (MBS).* The MBS approach occurs when no organization-wide consensus or clear-cut directives exist on which way to head and what to do. Each manager translates this to mean do your best to accomplish what you think should be done. This is a "do your own thing the best way you know how" approach. This is also referred to as "the mystery approach." Managers are left on their own with no clear direction ever articulated by senior management.

4. *Managing By Hope (MBH).* In this approach, decisions are predicated on the hope that they will work out and that good times are just around the corner. It is based on the belief that if you try hard enough and long enough, then things are bound to get better. Poor performance is attributed to unexpected events and the fact that decisions always have uncertainties and surprises. Much time is therefore spent hoping and wishing things will get better.

All four of these approaches represent "muddling through. Absent is any effort to calculate what is needed to influence where an organization is headed and what its activities should be to reach specific objectives. In contrast, managing by objectives is much more likely to achieve targeted results and have a sense of direction.

Characteristics of Good Objectives

For objectives to serve as a means of providing direction and as a standard for evaluation, they must possess certain characteristics. The more of these attributes possessed by a given objective, the more likely it will achieve its basic purpose. Sound objectives should have the following characteristics:

1. *Objectives should be clear and concise.* There should not be any room for misunderstanding what results are sought in a given objective. The use of long statements with words or phrases, which may be defined or interpreted in different ways by different people, should be avoided.

2. *Objectives should be in written form.* This helps to provide effective communication and to discourage the altering of unwritten objectives over time. Everyone realizes that oral statements can be unintentionally altered as they are communicated. Written statements avoid this problem and permit ease of communication. A second problem with unwritten objectives is that they tend to be altered to fit current circumstances.

3. *Objectives should name specific results in key areas.* The key areas in which objectives are needed will be identified later in this chapter. Specific desired results, such as "100,000 dollars in annual contributions" rather than a "high level of contributions" or "an acceptable level of contributions," should be used to avoid doubt about what result is sought.

4. *Objectives should be stated for a specific time period.* For example, objectives that are set for a short-run, more immediate time period such as six months to one year must be accomplished as a prerequisite to longer-run objectives. The time period specified becomes a deadline for producing results and also sets up the final evaluation of the success of a strategy.

5. *Objectives should be stated in measurable terms.* Concepts, which defy precise definition and qualification, should be avoided. "Goodwill" is an example of a concept which is important, but which in itself is difficult to define and measure. If a planner decides that goodwill is a concept, which must be measured, a substitute measure or measures will have to be used. An objective related to goodwill, which would be capable of quantification, might be stated as follows: "To have at least 85 percent of our constituents, rate our church as the best church in the area in our annual survey." Phrases such as "high attendance" not only are not clear or specific, but also cannot be measured. Does high mean first, second, or third in attendance? Is it a specific number or a percent? If the statement is quantified as "Increase attendance by 10 percent by December 1," it can be objectively measured. The accomplishment or failure of such a stated objective can be readily evaluated.

6. *Objectives must be consistent with overall organizational objectives and purpose.* This idea has been previously stated, but must be continually reemphasized because of the need for organizational unity.

7. *Objectives should be attainable, but of sufficient challenge to stimulate effort.* Two problems can be avoided if this characteristic is achieved. One is the avoidance of frustration produced by objectives which cannot be attained, or which cannot be attained within the specified time period. If an organization already has an unusually large attendance, the desirability

and likelihood of substantial increases in attendance are doubtful. The other problem is setting objectives, which are so easy to attain that only minimum effort is needed. This results in an unrealistic performance evaluation and does not maximize the contribution of a given strategic plan.

One approach to writing objectives, which contain these characteristics, is to apply a set of criteria to each statement to increase the probability of good objectives. One such list follows.

1. *Relevance*. Are the objectives related to and supportive of the basic purpose of the organization?

2. *Practicality*. Do the objectives take into consideration obvious constraints?

3. *Challenge*. Do the objectives provide a challenge?

4. *Measurability*. Are the objectives capable of some form of quantification, if only on an order-of-magnitude basis?

5. *Schedule*. Are the objectives so constituted that they can be time phased and monitored at interim points to ensure progress toward their attainment?

6. *Balance*. Do the objectives provide for a proportional emphasis, on all activities and keep the strengths and weaknesses of the organization in proper balance?

Objectives that meet such criteria are much more likely to serve their intended purpose. The resulting statements can then serve as the directing force in the development of strategy.

Consider the following examples of poorly-stated objectives:

Poor: Our objective is to maximize attendance.

> *How much is "maximum"? The statement is not subject to measurement. What criterion or yardstick will be used to determine if and when actual attendance is equal to the maximum? No deadline is specified.*

Better: Our objective is to achieve an attendance target for worship services in three years averaging 1000 per week.

Poor: Our objective is to increase contributions.

> *How much? A one-dollar increase will meet that objective, but is that really the desired target?*

Better: Our objective this calendar year is to increase contributions from 300,000 to 350,000 dollars.

Poor: Our objective is to boost advertising expenditures by 15 percent.

Advertising is an activity, not a result. The advertising objective should be stated in terms of what result the extra advertising is intended to produce.

Better: Our objective is to boost our viewing audience from 8 percent to 10 percent in the next five years with the help of a 15 percent increase in advertising expenditures.

Poor: Our objective is to be the best church in our area.

Not specific enough; what measures of "best" are to be used? Attendance? Contributions? New programs started? Services offered? Number of converts?

Better: We will strive to become the number-one church in the metropolitan area in terms of new converts baptized within five years.

Keep the following suggestions in mind when writing objectives (Hale 1984, .5-13):

1. Objectives should start with the word "to" followed by an action verb, since the achievement of an objective must come as a result of specific action;

2. Objectives should specify a single major result to be accomplished so the group will know precisely when the objective has been achieved;

3. An objective should have a target date for accomplishment;

4. The objective should relate directly to the mission statement of the group or individual. A parish council liturgy committee should not write an objective outside

5. The scope of its own mission statement or one that pertains more to the mission statement of the parish council. This may seem obvious, but groups often commit themselves to projects for which they have neither responsibility nor authority;

6. The objective must be understandable to those who will be working to achieve the specified results;

7. The objective must be possible to achieve;

8. The objective should be consistent with parish and diocesan policies and practices.

Types of Objectives Included in a Strategic Plan

Five-year objectives can be set in areas: such as attendance, programs offered, missionary support, building programs, and so forth. For example, "Key Result Areas" for setting objectives could include:

1. Level of membership

2. Level and sources of funds

3. Neighborhood acceptance

4. Youth participation

5. Quantity of programs

6. Quality of programs

7. Leadership effectiveness

8. Quantity and quality of services (McConkey 1978, 21)

Strategic plans for churches and ministries usually contain at least three types of objectives: attendance, (and/or listening/viewing), contributions, and constituents. Short-term objectives are stated for the operating period only, normally one year, whereas, long-term objectives usually span five to 20 years.

Attendance Objectives

Attendance or audience objectives relate to an organization's impact on an area, and are a basic measure of the level of activity for a program or service. Attendance objectives are closely tied to scheduling of services, budgeting, and so on.

Many people have difficulty with the emphasis on numbers and certainly if growing larger for the sake of "being big" is our motive, it is completely out of line with Biblical teachings. God deals with individuals; individuals make commitments, help others, serve, etc. However, a different perspective can, also be used for the emphasis on numbers.

The pastor of a newly formed church in a small town in Arkansas made a couple of insightful statements about numbers. The church meets at a Days Inn because it has no building. The pastor's brother is associate pastor and music director and both their wives play instruments and/or sing in the services. Sunday school for youth and children is held in motel rooms. After only four months of existence the church already had attendance in excess of 100 several times with a theme of "Everyone Bring One." The pastor explained the theme by stating that people have to be reached; an empty chair has never been saved, made a commitment, helped others, or asked for prayer. He went on to say that if the church is spreading the Gospel and meeting people's needs, it will grow; and if it is not it should not be here.

Attendance objectives may be stated numerically or as a percent of the total number. If the objectives are stated in percents, they also need to be converted to numbers for budgeting and estimating the audience size. Examples of attendance objectives are given in Exhibit 5-1. The way objectives are stated must reflect what the organization can realistically expect to attain under a given plan. Also, the steps of setting objectives and developing strategy in preparing a marketing plan should be viewed as interactive. In setting objectives, we first state them in terms of what we want to accomplish, but as we develop the strategy we may discover that we cannot afford what we want. The available resources committed to a given program or service may not be sufficient to achieve a stated objective; and if the planning process is resource-controlled, the objectives must be altered. It must be remembered that objectives are not fate, but they are direction. They are not commands, but they become commitments. As a planner, you must not fall into the trap of thinking that once objectives are set they cannot be altered.

Each of the objectives in Exhibit 5-1 is clear, concise, quantifiable, and stated within a given time period. Only objective 2 requires external data to evaluate whether it was accomplished. Total audience size would be required to compute the percentage.

EXHIBIT 5-1
Examples of Attendance-Oriented Objectives
1.   Achieve average attendance of 500 for Sunday School within three years.
2.   Have 50 percent of the potential TV audience view our annual Christmas special this year.

Contribution Objectives

Contributions are a vital part of any church or ministry.

While they are never ends in themselves, they are the enabling resources that are needed by an organization. However, there is a more practical reason for including a specific statement about contributions: it forces the planner to estimate the resources needed to underwrite specific programs and services. A statement of whether resources will be available cannot be made without at least some analysis of the cost of providing services for activities which must break even. For new programs, the expenditures and contributions associated with the program should have been analyzed before introduction. For existing programs, contributions can be analyzed to project continued levels of support. This information, combined with estimates of expenses involved in implementing the marketing strategy, provides a basis for statements of objectives about contributions.

Sample statements are shown in Exhibit 5-2 as illustrations of contribution objectives. Again, nebulous statements such as "acceptable contribution levels" or "reasonable contributions" should be avoided because of the possible variations in definition and the lack of quantifiability. The objective of a percentage increase in contributions is the only one requiring additional information for its evaluation. The amount of the total previous contribution would be required to determine whether this objective has been reached.

EXHIBIT 5-2
Examples of Contribution Objectives
1. Produce net contributions of 180,000 dollars by year five.
2. Generate a 20 percent increase in contributions within five years.
3. Produce a contribution of 85,000 dollars for the summer youth camp, within three years.

Keep in mind that the interactive processes of setting objectives and developing strategies must be used to set objectives that are realistic. The costs of many aspects of strategy cannot be estimated until a written statement of strategy is developed. If the strategy calls for a new program, for example, that strategy must be spelled out in detail before costs can be estimated.

Constituent Objectives

Constituent objectives may seem unusual to some, but their inclusion should be obvious. They serve as enabling objectives in attendance and contributions, and also represent specific statements of constituent behaviors and/or attitudes an organization would want members to have toward its programs and services.

Constituent objectives are especially important in providing direction to the development of the strategy section of the plan. As shown in Exhibit 5-3, they specify results desired of constituents in terms of behaviors and attitudes, and should have the same characteristics as other objectives. They must be stated in objectively measurable terms and should be evaluated in relation to their accomplishment as a part of the monitoring and control system used in the plan.

EXHIBIT 5-3
Examples of Constituent **Objectives**
1. Create at least 20 percent participation in our new missions program within a three year period.
2. Have at least 80 percent of our members rate the quality of our programs as "very good" in our annual survey of members.

Using Environmental Analysis Data to Set Objectives

The objectives of a given plan are based on the data provided in the analysis discussed earlier. In other words, good objectives are based on a careful analysis of the external and internal environment of the church or ministry. A specific example of how data are used in setting objectives may help in understanding this point.

A large church in a city of approximately 400,000 people had a very low and declining number of youth age 13 to 18. The church had a youth facility capable of handling up to 300 young people. The environmental factors were, for the most part, favorable, and the total youth population had a healthy growth rate.

The analysis, identified three market segments for youth services, one of which was: for after-school activities. This was a unique segment with special needs in terms of transportation, types of services and facilities desired, and timing of the events.

The number of youth was found in public records available through the school system, and the number interested in afterschool programs was estimated through a telephone survey of a sample of 50 youths. The resulting analysis is shown in Exhibit 5-4.

Objectives derived through such a process represent the realities of the area and also the church's willingness and ability to, commit itself to such objectives. This example should also reemphasize the logic in the strategic planning format. The analysis precedes the setting of objectives, because realistic objectives must be derived from the results of the analysis.

Performance Contracts

Objectives can become the basis of a performance contract for staff members. As an example, note how the objectives for an associate pastor can become a performance contract through the following process:

1. Properly written objectives submitted to the pastor

2. Items discussed and negotiated with the pastor

3. Objectives resubmitted to the pastor

4. List approved by both parties (and perhaps the pastor/parish relations committee)

5. In some organizations, both parties sign an objectives sheet

EXHIBIT 5-4
Potential for After-School Youth **Program**

1. Population in metropolitan area = 400,000

2. Number of youth in metropolitan area (13-18 years old) = 37,200

3. Number of youth within church's primary market area = 3,000

4. Percent of youth in telephone survey who say they are interested in after-school programs at church = 10 percent (i.e., five out of 50 called)

5. Total number of youth who represent a viable target = 300 (i.e. 3,000 x .10)

6. Objective: Attract an average of 300 youths per week within three years.

Periodic Review

One practical, easy way to record, communicate, measure, and update objectives is through a "Performance Plan Book" or "Management Plan Book." All objectives for the organization should be in this book. Objectives are to be reviewed each quarter and updated. Shown below are examples of how objectives can be listed, tracked, and presented for review. This process greatly reduces paperwork and provides a convenient method for review. Examples are of overall church objectives that encourage a look into the future. They take into account key result areas and suggestions by more than 50 pastors and scholars.

Overall Church Objectives, 1996-1998

	2014	2015	2016
Staff			
Pastor			
Assistants			
Attendance			
First services			
Second services			
Sunday School			
Sunday night			
Wednesday night			
Revivals			
Training seminars			
Membership			

Buildings			
Build a new church			
Facilities improvement			
Added equipment			
Missions Outreach			
Contribution (to central fund)			
Other mission trips			
Annual Mexico trips			
Calling (lay) people involved			
Number of calls			
Evangelism			
Hospital			
Post-hospital			
Inactive			
Home department			
Nursing homes			
Facilities			
Annual safety check			
Sound system			
Heating and cooling			
Burglar alarms			
Lighting			
Parking			
Programs			
Children			
Youth			
Young adults, college age			
Men, women, senior citizens			
Divorce recovery			
Widowed			
Alcoholic recovery			
Marriage enrichment			
Caring calling			
Family life			
Political and social action			
Lay ministry training			

People/Training Morale			
House training per staff Retreat days for minister Retreat days for laity Retreats Yearly attitude survey Small groups: types, number Counseling participants Ministerial Lay Alcoholics, drug abusers Divorcees/widows			
Public Responsibility			
Use facilities for civic club lunches Sponsor Boy Scout and Girl Scout troop Social service Relief Talking books Prison ministry Meals-on-wheels Personal growth Initiate daily devotions Attend growth seminars			
Financial			
Average collections (per service) Budget Current ratio New tithers New pledgers Stewardship of persons New persons accepting responsibility New lay ministers New candidates for ordained ministry Fixed asset turnover/collections/ net fixed assets Total asset turnover/collections/ total assets Debt ratio/total debt/total assets Debt/total collections Times interest earned/collections/ interest			

Review Sheet Management Plan, 1996

1. Routine

    Set aside 5,000 dollars For overseas missions programs throughout
    every month of 1996
    On target

2. Problem Solving

    Develop an efficient transportation routing schedule to be followed by the
    bus outreach captains by March 31, 1996

    Met 90 percent

3. Innovative

    Devise a better layout for member parking during

    February 1996

    Done

4. Personal

    Read the book MBO: Blue Collar to Top Executive, attend Communication
    Course, Fall of 1996

5. Budget Performance

    Operate within the 50,000 dollar church budget throughout fiscal 1996

    On target

Church Administrator's Objectives, 1996

1. Routine

    Make at least one hospital visit per week
    Exercise four times per week
    Review each committee chair's objectives and accomplishments by January
       5, May 5, and August 5
    Attend the annual state pastors' meeting

2. Problem-Solving

    Develop, a project for the 11- to 14-year-old youth to make a contribution to
       the community
    Develop youth minister internship plan with local pastors by January 31

Develop, a set of criteria and measurable objectives for the Sunday school retreat

Hold a one-day symposium on the spiritual and mental health of young people; prepare summary minutes and recommendations, for improvement within three years

3. Innovative

Devise a better system of screening prospective church employees

Develop a method or methods to give all committee chairs feedback on their budget performance. At least one method to be implemented by May 1, and another method implemented by June 1, 1998

4. Personal

Improve my understanding of the Bible (I will read three pages per day and attend at least one Bible-study group.)

Do not miss one Sunday service

5. Team

Work with the organist on revision and update of hymnbook to be introduced in July

Meet with the pastor each Wednesday to coordinate the music with the sermon

6. Budget

Operate within the 100,000 dollar yearly budget

Retire 10 percent of the debt on the church building

Summary

Setting objectives is another major part of the strategic planning process. The necessity for objectives as well as their characteristics was presented here to lay the groundwork for identifying basic types of objectives, such as attendance, contributions, and constituents. The objectives provided as examples in this chapter can be used both as a source of direction and to evaluate the strategies developed in the plan.

Objectives Worksheet

This worksheet will aid you in applying the concepts discussed in this chapter to your church or ministry.

Answer These Questions First

1. What do your objectives need to relate to-attendance, contributions, constituents or all three? What about other key result areas?

2. What needs to happen for your program to be successful? In other words, how many people need to attend/watch, join, contribute, volunteer, etc.?

3. When do you want this to happen? By what specific date?

Now Write your Objectives

Use the information in your answers to these three questions to write statements of your objectives.

Objective 1:

_____

_____

_____

Objective 2:

_____

_____

_____

Objective 3:

_____

_____

_____

Now test each statement using the criteria given in this chapter. Is each statement relevant to the basic purpose of your organization? Is each statement practical? Does each statement provide a challenge? Is each statement stated in objectively measurable terms? Do you have a specific date for completion? Does each statement contribute to a balance of activities in line with your church's strengths and weaknesses?

References

Drucker, Peter F. *The Practice of Management.* New York: Harper & Row, 1954.

McConkey, Dale D. *Goal Setting: A Guide to Achieving the Church's Mission.* Minneapolis: Augsburg Pub. Co., 1978.

Thompson, Arthur A., and A. J. Strickland. *Strategy Formulation and Implementation: Tasks of the General Manager.* 3rd ed. Plano, Tex.: Business Publications, 1986.

Chapter 6
Developing Strategy and Operational Plans

> *May he give you the desire of your heart and make all your plans succeed.*
> —*Proverbs 20:4*

After developing a set of objectives for the time period covered by the strategic plan, you must formulate the strategy needed to accomplish those objectives. You must first design an overall strategy. Then you must plan the operating details of that strategy, as it relates to providing ministry services, promotion, determining location, and enlisting contributions, to guide the church's efforts. In this chapter we introduce the concept of strategy and describe strategy elements and approaches to strategy development.

Strategy Concepts

The word "strategy" has been used in a number' of ways over the years, especially in the context of business. Often, it is confused with the terms "objectives," "policies,." "procedures," "strategies," and "tactics." Strategy may be defined as the course of action taken by an organization to achieve its objectives. It is the catalyst or dynamic element of managing which enables a company to accomplish its objectives.

Strategy development is both a science and an art and is a product of both logic and creativity. The scientific aspect deals with assembling and allocating the resources necessary to achieve an organization's objectives with emphasis on opportunities, costs, and time. The art of strategy is mainly concerned with the utilization of resources, including motivation of the people, sensitivity to the environment, and ability to adapt to changing conditions.

Alternate Strategies

The alternate strategies considered by management are the alternate courses of action evaluated by management before committing to a specific course of action outlined in the strategic plan. Thus, strategy is the link between objectives and results.

There are two basic strategies a church or ministry can use to accomplish its objectives: a differentiated strategy and focus strategy. The chosen strategy must of course be an outgrowth of the organization's basic purpose.

Differentiated Strategy

A differentiated strategy is a strategy that entails developing services that are aimed at meeting a broad spectrum of needs. It is the strategy used by most churches that develop a whole gamut of programs. Research has shown that this is the best strategy for new churches in terms of generating increases in membership.

First Baptist Church of West Monroe, Louisiana uses this strategy. The church offers a wide variety of ministry programs.

Preschool and Children's Ministry

The areas of ministry involved are: (1) Christian education, through Sunday morning study; (2) special education, providing Bible learning activities for mentally handicapped children and youth; and (3) vacation Bible school, provided ,each summer.

Youth Ministry (7th through 12th grades, or Junior High and High School)

The areas of ministry involved are: (I) Christian education through Sunday morning Bible study; (2) discipleship through Church Training each Sunday night and Disciple Now, a special weekend emphasis each year; and (3) special activities such as Agape House which is open on weekends for youth fellowship, witness training, snow skiing, summer camp, fall recreates, fellowships, banquets, recreational activities, special bible studies, and music.

Single Adult Ministry (includes never married, divorced, or widowed)

The areas of ministry involved are: (1) Christian education through Sunday morning Bible Study, and Sunday evening services; and (2) social activities including fellowship times at church and in homes, trips, special entertainment, retreats, and conferences.

Music Ministry

The areas of ministry involved are: choirs, vocal ensembles, and bell choirs spanning preschool, children, junior and senior high, and adults.

Recreation Ministry

The areas of ministry involving all age groups are: (1) sports, including teams and individuals, instructional classes, and church-wide tournaments; (2) Christian outdoor experiences, including group retreats, day and mission camps, youth camps, and other outdoor activities; and (3) crafts and continuing education classes.

Outreach Ministry

The areas of ministry involved are: (1) venture revivals, in area churches by lay members; (2) special projects in missions, such as construction or renovation of mission churches or facilities; (3) missionary home, for Baptist missionaries home on furlough; and (4) visitation on a regular schedule.

By using a differentiated strategy, First Baptist Church thus targets a broad· segment of markets ranging across preschool, children, youth, singles, families, adults, senior citizens, handicapped, etc.

Focus Strategy

A focus strategy is more likely to be used by a ministry because it involves concentrating on the needs of a specific group or on a specific type of ministry. Missions to Mexico, headquartered in Pharr, Texas, uses this strategy. Brother Edgar Stone has devoted his life's ministry to taking the Gospel to areas where there is no current work by any other Christian group. He has basically created a ministry that involves bringing in converts who feel a call to be pastors and putting them through a two-year educational program similar to seminary training. He then encourages these new pastors to return to their villages and he helps them to start a new church by paying up to one half of the construction cost. This has resulted in the construction of over 150 churches in Mexico over the last 30 years.

While Missions to Mexico may occasionally be involved in other forms of ministry, such as summer youth camps for the youth of the churches established through the ministry, its main thrust is equipping pastors and building new churches.

The main advantages of this strategy are: (1) It capitalizes on the distinctive competencies of the people involved; and (2) It concentrates on doing one thing well. These advantages can also create a knowledge base of how to carry out certain types of ministry as well as improved efficiency in performing the ministry.

Factors Influencing the Strategy Selected

At least four factors influence the choice of a strategy selected by the firm: the organization's resources, the distinctive competencies of leaders and members, stage in the organization's life cycle, and strategies used by other organizations. There is no one best strategy, which will always prove successful. Instead, the strategy that is chosen must be the one that is best for the church or ministry, given the nature of these four factors. Resources, for example, may limit the organization to a focus strategy. The organization may even be an innovator in terms of ideas but not have the financial, communication, or personnel resources to offer other services.

As was emphasized in Chapter 2, the organization strategy must be derived from the organizational purpose and objectives. If the organizational purpose is focused on serving needs of diverse groups then the strategy used must be one that is compatible. In other words, what an organization *does* must be a function of what it *is*.

The distinctive competencies of the organization have a direct bearing on the strategy selected. Distinctive skills and experience in missions, for example, can influence strategy choice. These distinctive competencies are the basis of doing things well.

The organization's life-cycle stage is an additional factor influencing strategy selection. For example, an organization may begin with a focus strategy but add programs over time which serves more varied needs. Repositioning the organization through introducing new programs or serving new markets would be a pivotal point of the strategy.

The strategy selected must be given sufficient time to be implemented and affect groups served, but an obviously ineffective strategy should be changed. This concept should be understood without mention, but the resistance to change in many organizations is a common phenomenon.

Operational Plans

After all the steps have been taken and a strategy has been developed to meet your objectives and goals, it is time to create an operational or action plan. The operational plan is the "action" or "doing" stage. Here you hire, fire, build, advertise, and so on. How many times has a group of people planned something, become enthusiastic about it, and then nothing happened? This is usually because group leaders did not complete an operational or action plan to implement their strategy.

Operational plans must be developed in all the areas that are used to support the overall strategy. These include production, communication, finance, and staffing. Each of these more detailed plans is designed to spell out what needs to happen in a given area to implement the strategic plan.

The production plan identifies exactly what services will be provided to a specific group and the exact nature of those services. Will it be preaching, teaching, music, worship, or a combination of these activities? If a church is trying to launch mission work in an urban area of low income people, the work could take many forms. It could be a "satellite" church, a literacy' program, or it could concentrate on housing and feeding the homeless. These, of course, are completely different types of activities and must be carefully planned.

The communication plan is used to communicate the nature of the program, location, and time to the intended audience and also to the rest of the church. The plan also needs to be well thought out and carefully analyzed to avoid a lack of communication or miscommunication.

For example, Christ Is The Answer, located in El Paso, Texas, in developing their operational plans, needed a communication strategy to provide information to people about their purpose and programs. The communication strategy involved three key elements: informing, persuading, and reminding.

1. Informing—This involves providing information to individuals and groups about the organizations. Specific elements of this plan call for:

    -   use of video cassette presentations
    -   newsletters, pamphlets, and prayer guides
    -   personal speaking appearances by ministry leaders
    -   hosting luncheons/dinners sponsored by supporters
    -   on-site visits by individual groups to headquarters or ministry centers.

2. Persuading—This involves presenting the gospel message contained in the Great Commission as well as the principles from the apostle Paul's writings about the support he received while involved in mission work.

    -   Prepare application forms with which partners may request additional information or may apply as a team member.
    -   Provide opportunities for support by individuals through prayers and specific offerings for teams, supplies, and so forth.

3. Reminding—This aspect of the strategy is to continue to provide information to people already familiar with the ministry so they will be constantly reminded of the work and needs of the ministry:

    -   Send letters/newsletters and other materials regularly.
    -   Provide opportunities for team members to write supporters and future team members on a periodic basis.
    -   Develop a complete file of individuals and organizations by name for future mailings.

In the staffing plan you must identify who will carry out the activities involved. Will it be church/ministry staff or volunteers? If paid staff are to be used, will they be full-time or part-time? Of course, if volunteers are to be used, they must be recruited, trained and supervised. Since most churches must rely on the laity to carry' out plans, it may be necessary to develop a recruitment plan just to staff the activity.

Finances must also be planned. This is usually done in the form of a financial budget. The budget is the means to execute the plan. If the financial means to support the plan are not available you must adjust the objectives. There is a constant interplay between the budget and the plan. Many people do not understand the budgeting process. The budget is a tool. Too often, however, the budget becomes the "tail wagging the dog." "We budgeted it so we had better spend it," or "We had better add a little to this year's budget" are statements that reflect this misunderstanding. Budget money must be tied directly to performance, and performance is measured against objectives. Key results and objectives in a church and ministry are prioritized, and then money and resources are allocated.

An example of this interplay came out of a meeting at a large church. Most of their resources for the next two years would have to go into finishing current building programs. Only enough money was available to maintain the status quo of the church school even though they wanted to expand it. That does not mean the school is not important—it is—but the timing for expansion and growth for the school cannot come until the other projects are completed.

The action plan for a large church with many different types of programs and ministries i depicted in Exhibit 6-1 and 6-2. The operational or action plan in this example is related directly to the strategy to be used and the objectives to be accomplished in a step-by-step fashion. This forces the planner to align objectives, strategies, and action plans.

EXHIBIT 6-1

Action Plan: Home Groups

OBJECTIVE

To have 150 home groups in the next five years (1994-1998).
1994: 30 home groups
1995: 45 home groups
1996: 62 home groups
1997: 95 home groups
1998: 150 home groups

STRATEGIES

We plan to increase year by year as the total congregation grows so that we will be able to accommodate one-third to one-half of the congregation.
We plan to add one home group pastor for every 50 home groups.
Action Plan
Person Responsible
Start Date
Date Completed

Pastor Brooks is training several hand-picked couples as future home-group leaders. Each present home-group leader is in the process of training an assistant leader. Each existing home group, plus all new home groups are to set a goal to split and become two groups each year. They are to begin training an assistant within their new home group.

EXHIBIT 6-2

Action Plan: Children's Ministry

OBJECTIVE

    To have 500 children attending full children's Church services
during each of two adult morning services:

        1994—300
        1995—350
        1996—400
        1997—450
        1998—500

STRATEGIES

    Develop complete teacher-recruitment training program
    Develop neighborhood outreach ministry for children
    Develop teacher training program
    Develop puppet ministry
    Hire full-time children's pastor

        Person Responsible
        Start Date
        Action Plan
        Date Completed

Hire part-time pastor

Establish teacher training course and teacher recruitment strategy.

Begin Saturday advertising campaign in community.

Conduct four, picnic-type outings a year to attract local children.

Hire full-time children's pastor.

Puppet ministry in two services.

Update training services.

Notice that the Action Plan format takes one objective out of the five-year strategic plan and isolates it for further study and analysis. In this case it shows the targets at which this church is aiming with its Home Groups and Children's Ministry. You never go into action until the target is clear and understood by everyone. It is important that all those who execute these plans be in on the planning and be aware of what is going on. That is the key to enthusiasm and support by the people. With targets/objectives/goals in mind, the various strategies are agreed upon. They are listed immediately under the objectives. Next, all the actions that must take place are listed. Also note that at the top of each section is a row to write who is in charge, date started, and date completed. This document becomes not only a guide to action but also a timeline for starting and completing plans.

The person or persons responsible and the expected date of completion must be agreed upon. Every person involved gets a copy of the plan with his/her areas of responsibility marked.

Now, one person can coordinate a multitude of projects and programs, because there is a clear record of what is to be done. As each action or task is completed, the person responsible sends in a completion report. With this approach, the coordinator knows what is going on all the time.

The action plan is periodically updated so that everyone sees the progress. After people become accustomed to using the Action Plan format, they discipline themselves. They do not want others to see that they are falling behind. This is a great time-saving and coordinating format. In Appendix C we present a sample strategic plan for Calvary Temple of Temple Terrace to illustrate the development of strategies to accomplish a mission.

Summary

A well-thought-out plan developed by everyone succeeds.

How many times do you see churches and ministries trying to do everything at once? The word "strategies" in the title of this book implies thinking, praying, and seeking order. All this can happen if an Action Plan coordinates and supports the overall plan.

Strategy Development Worksheet

This worksheet is provided to help you apply the concepts discussed in this chapter to your church or ministry.

Answer These Questions First

What are the distinctive competencies of your church/ministry? What do you do well?

_____

_____

_____

What market segment or segments should you select to match your church/ministry's skills and resources and constituents' needs in those segments?

_____

_____

_____

Do you have the skills/resources to pursue several segments or should you concentrate on one segment? Is that segment large enough to sustain your church/ministry and allow for growth?

_____

_____

_____

Now Develop your Positioning Statement

Distinctive Competencies

_____

_____

_____

Segments Sought

_____

_____

_____

Services Offered

_____

_____

_____

Promotion Orientation

_____

_____

_____

Contribution Levels

_____

_____

_____

Growth Orientation

_____

_____

_____

Chapter 7
Evaluation and Control Procedures

Watch out that you do not lose what you have worked for, but that
you may be rewarded fully.
—2 John 1:8

The evaluation and control stage of the strategic planning process can be compared to setting out on a journey with a road map. The process includes identifying your destination (objective), determining the best route to your destination (strategy), and then departing for your trip (implementation of your strategy): During the journey, you look for highway signs (feedback) to tell you if you are on the way to your objective. Signs along the way quickly reveal if you have made a wrong turn, and you can alter your course to get back on the right road. When you reach your destination, you decide on a new route (strategy) to get you somewhere else.

Imagine what would happen if there were no road signs during your trip to let you know if you were on the right road. It might be too late to continue the trip by the time you realized you were traveling in the wrong direction. Yet, many churches are involved in a similar situation, failing to analyze results to determine if objectives are being accomplished.

Failure to establish procedures to appraise and control the strategic plan can lead to less than optimal performance. Many organizations fail to understand the importance of establishing procedures to appraise and control the planning process. In this chapter we review the need for evaluation and control, what is to be controlled, and some control procedures. Evaluation and control should be a natural follow-through in developing a plan (see Chapter 2). No plan should be considered complete until controls are identified and the procedures for recording and transmitting control information to administrators of the plan are established.

Integration of Planning and Control

Planning and control should be integral processes. In fact, planning was defined as a process that included establishing a system for feedback of results. This feedback reflects the organization's performance in reaching its objectives through implementation of the strategic plan. The relationship between planning and control is depicted in Exhibit 7-1.

EXHIBIT 7-1 Planning and Control Process

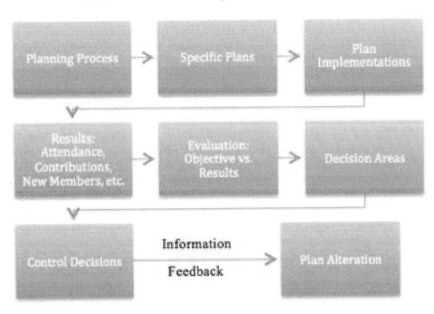

The strategic planning process results in a strategic plan.

This plan is implemented (activities are performed in the manner described in the plan) and results are produced. These results include such things as attendance, contributions, and accompanying constituent attitudes, preferences, and behaviors. Information on these results and other key result areas is given to administrators, who compare the results with objectives to evaluate performance. In this performance evaluation they identify the areas where decisions must be made to adjust activities, people, or finances. Through this decision making the administrators control the plan by altering it to accomplish stated objectives, and a new cycle begins. The information flows are the key to a good control system.

The last stage of the strategic planning process, then, is to appraise the church and each of its entities to determine if all objectives have been met.

- Have the measurable objectives and goals been accomplished?

- How far did actual performance miss the mark? Did the attainment of the objectives and goals, support the overall purpose?

- Has the environment changed enough to change the objectives and goals?

- Have additional weaknesses been revealed that will influence changing the objectives of the organization?

- Have additional strengths been added or your position improved sufficiently to influence the changing of your objectives?

- Has the ministry, provided its members with organizational rewards, both extrinsic and intrinsic?

- Is there a feedback system to help members satisfy their high level needs?

Timing of Information Flows

The strategic plan is supported by operational plans. If each of our operational plans is controlled properly, the strategic plans are more likely to be controlled. The administrator cannot afford to wait for the time period of a plan to pass before control information is available. The information must be available within a time frame, which is long enough to allow results to accrue, but short enough to allow actions to align results with objectives. Although some types of organizations may find weekly or bimonthly results necessary, most organizations can adequately control operations with monthly or quarterly reports. Cumulative monthly or quarterly reports become annual reports, which in turn become the feedback needed to control the plan. Deciding what information is provided to which administrators in what time periods is the essence of a control system.

Performance Evaluation and Control

Performance should be evaluated in many areas to provide a complete analysis of what the results are and what caused them. Three key control areas are attendance, contributions, and constituents' attitudes. Objectives should have been established in all of these areas for the strategic plan.

Attendance Control

Attendance or audience control data are provided from an analysis of attendance for individual programs or services. Attendance can be evaluated on a program-by-program basis by developing a performance report as shown in Exhibit 7-2. When such a format is used, the attendance objectives stated in the plan are broken down on a quarterly basis and become the standard against which actual attendance results are compared. Number and percentage variations are calculated, because in some instances a small percentage can result in a large number variation.

A performance index can be calculated by dividing actual attendance by the attendance objective. Index numbers near 1.00 indicate that expected and actual performance are about equal.

Numbers larger than 1.00 indicate above-expected performance, and numbers below 1.00 reveal below-expected performance.

Index numbers are especially useful when a large number of programs are involved, because they enable administrators to identify those programs which need immediate attention.

EXHIBIT 7-2				
Attendance **and** Performance **Report** Quarter **1 (By** Program)				
Program	**A**	**B**	**C**	**D**
Attendance Objective	1000	950	1200	2000
Actual Attendance	900	1020	920	2030
Variation	100	+70	−280	+30
% Variation	−10.0	+7.4	−23.0	+1.5
Performance Index	.90	1.07	77	1.02

Contribution/Cost Controls

Several tools are available for establishing cost control procedures, including budgets, expense ratios, and activity costs analysis. Budgets are a common tool used by many organizations for both planning and control. The budget is often established by using historical percentages of various expenses as a percent of sales. Thus, once the total level of expected contributions is established, expense items can be budgeted as a percent of total sales. If zero-based budgeting is used, the objectives to be accomplished must be specified and the expenditures necessary to accomplish these objectives estimated. The estimates are the budgeted expenses for the time period.

Contributions are controlled by tracing gifts on a weekly or at least a monthly basis. While many organizations have an annual drive for pledges, others are continually seeking contributions from constituents. A prerequisite to controlling contributions is an annual projection of operating expenses. This projection, broken down on a quarterly or monthly basis, becomes the standard from which deviations are analyzed. For example, a church with a projected budget of 500,000 dollars for the next fiscal year would be expecting about 125,000 dollars per quarter, or 41,667 dollars per month.

If there were large variations related to certain times of the year, even the variations can be analyzed to determine the proportion of the budgeted amount given per month. If, historically, 20 percent of the budget was given during December, then 20 percent of next year's budget becomes the expected level of contributions to be used as the standard.

The same type of analysis used to control attendance (Exhibit 7-2) can be used to analyze data on contributions. This type of analysis should be performed on a timely basis to enable expansion or cutbacks of programs when contribution levels go above or below the expected amounts for the period.

Once the budget is established, expense variance analysis by line item or expenditure category is used to control costs. A typical procedure is to prepare monthly or quarterly budget reports showing the amount budgeted for the time period and the dollar and percentage variation from the budgeted amount, if any exists. Expenditure patterns, which vary from the budgeted amounts, are then analyzed to determine why the variations occurred.

Larger churches find revenue/expense centers to be a useful tool for control. For example, a church tape ministry generates revenues through the sale of tapes and incurs costs in recording, duplicating, and mailing out tapes; overhead; and labor costs. Tracking these revenues and expenses in a cost center would help control this ministry by letting the administrator know if it is breaking even or if it is generating excess revenues which could be used to expand the ministry or to lower the price of the tapes.

Constituent Feedback

The final area of performance evaluation is constituents, and involves analysis of awareness, knowledge, attitudes, and behaviors of members, participants, or supporters. Every organization should want its constituents to become aware of programs, services, or personnel; possess certain knowledge; and exhibit certain attitudes and behaviors. If these are specified in the objective statements, these objectives are the standards to which current constituent data are compared.

Data on constituents must be collected on a regular basis. There are many ways to collect data but annual surveys are commonly used.

Constituent data are especially valuable if collected over a long period of time, because awareness levels, satisfaction, attitudes, and behavior can be analyzed to reveal trends and areas for further investigation.

Establishing Procedures

None of the performance evaluation data described are going to be available unless they are requested and funds are made available to finance them. Thus, data collecting and reporting procedures must be set up by the administrators who are going to use the control data in decision making.

The procedures will usually change over time as new types of analysis or reporting times are found to be better than others. The most important requirement is that the data meet the needs of administrators in taking corrective actions to control activities. With the expanded availability and use of computers by churches and ministries, much of the work can be computerized.

Performance Evaluation Guidelines

Keep these summary guidelines in mind when establishing an effective, system for performance evaluation:

A. Performance evaluation must be self-evaluation;
B. Performance evaluation is for healthy, performing, growing individuals;
C. Evaluation is subjective;
D. "No evaluation" is not an option;
E. When an evaluation process is perceived as legitimate, fair, and working, people will tend to use it responsibly. When it is not, people will still do something, but they may not feel the burden of responsibility;
F. Performance evaluation is a formal process.

It is in the appraisal and control stage that churches and ministries really begin to see the benefits of the strategic concepts outlined in this book. When people at all levels know the progress being made toward fulfilling the overall plan, it creates a sense of pride, accomplishment, and excitement. Strategic planning will not work well without a review of performance.

Summary

No planning process should be considered complete until appraisal and control procedures have been established. Performance evaluation is vital for control decisions. Information tells an administrator what has happened, and serves as the basis for any actions needed to control the activities of the organization toward predetermined objectives. Without such information, it is impossible to manage marketing activities with any sense of clarity about what is actually happening in the organization.

Evaluation and Control Worksheet

This worksheet will aid you in applying the concepts discussed in this chapter to your church or' ministry.

Answer the Following Questions

1. What kind of information do you need to evaluate a program's or service's success?

2. Who should receive and review this information?

3. What time periods do you want to use to analyze the data? Weekly? Monthly?

4. What record keeping system do you need to devise to make sure the information you want is recorded for the time periods you specified in question 3?

NOW SET UP YOUR CONTROL PROCEDURES

1. Specify the areas to be controlled:

   A. _____
   B. _____
   C. _____
   D. _____

2. Specify the format of the data for each area. (Is it to be numbers by month by program? Do you want number and percentage variations?)

   A. _____
   B. _____
   C. _____
   D. _____

3. Specify how the data are to be collected, who is to collect and analyze the data, and who is to receive the results of the analysis:

   A. How will the data be collected?
   B. Who has responsibility to correct and analyze the data?
   C. Who is to receive which type of analysis?

Administrator/Pastor	Types of Analysis
1. _____	1. _____
2. _____	2. _____
3. _____	3. _____
4. _____	4. _____

Appendix A
Church and Ministry Strategic and Management Planning Worksheets

1. Purpose

    What is your reason for being, your mission, why you are needed; customers served; needs met in marketplace; scope of the endeavor; nationwide, local; ethics; profit, or nonprofit.

    Where there is no vision, the people perish: but he that keepeth the law, happy is he.
    Proverbs 29:18

    And it shall come to pass afterward, that I will pour out my spirit upon all flesh; and your sons and your daughters shall prophesy, your old men shall dream dreams, your young men shall see visions. . .
    Joel 2:28

2. Environmental Analysis

    It is the glory of God to conceal a thing: but the honour of kings is to search out a matter.
    Proverbs 25:2

3. Strengths and Weaknesses (usually internal)

    A. Human
    B. Facilities/Equipment
    C. Programs
    D. Financial
    E. Communication

    But he that knew not, and did commit things worthy of stripes, shall be beaten with few stripes. For unto whomsoever much is given, of him shall be much required: and to whom men have committed much, of him they will ask the more.
    Luke 12:48

    That the man of God may be perfect, thoroughly furnished unto all good works.
    2 Timothy 3:17

4.   Assumptions

    A.   You have no control over

      1. _____

      2. _____

      3. _____

    B.   Extend environmental analysis

      1. _____

      2. _____

      3. _____

    C.   Usually external

      1. _____

      2. _____

      3. _____

5.   Objectives and Goals

Specific, time frame, measurable in key result areas.

	Last Year	Next Year	Five Years
Attendance			
Membership			
Building			
Missions			
Facilities			
Programs			
Financial			
People			

Let all things be done decently and in order.
   I Corinthians 14:40

Then the King said unto me, For what dost thou make request? So I prayed to the God of heaven.
   Nehemiah 2:4

Now, for each key result area, use this format to develop specific objectives, strategies and actions.

Key Result Area
Objective

Strategy to achieve objective:

1. _____

2. _____

3. _____

What I have to do to make it happen:

1. _____

2. _____

3. _____

Strategy—Two to three strategies for each objective

A. Thinking stage

B. Where and how to commit resources

C. Timing

Neither do men light a candle, and put it under a bushel, but on a candlestick; and it giveth light unto all that are in the house.
  Matthew 5:15

Problems

Major: _____

Minor: _____

Analysis
Alternatives

1. _____

2. _____

3. _____

Recommendations

Operational Plan

A.   Getting work accomplished

B.   Budget

C.   What is the budget for key departments?

Department, Last Year, This Year, Next Year (Projected)

Let all things be done decently and in order.
  I Corinthians 14:40

Study to shew thyself approved unto God, a workman that needeth not to be ashamed, rightly dividing the word of truth.
  2 Timothy 2:15

For which of you, intending to build a tower, sitteth not down first and counteth the cost, whether he have sufficient to finish it?
  Luke 14:28

Reward/Performance Appraisal

A.   Agreed upon objectives

B.   Review of performance

C.

Now he that planteth and he that watereth are one: and every man shall receive his own reward according to his own labour.
  I Corinthians 3:8

**Set Up A Way To Monitor How You Are Doing & A Way
To Create Action**

An action plan for each objective area should be developed. The action plan puts objectives, strategies, and operational plans into perspective with each other and helps you develop the inter-relationships between the phases. It helps goals come to life with appropriate action

Action Plan Objective:

Action Plan			
Person Responsible			
Start Date			
Date Completed			

Strategies

A. _____

B. _____

C. _____

D. _____

E. _____

Appendix B:
Church Ministry: Strategic Marketing Plan

Church/Ministry Strategic Marketing Plan to Support the Church/Ministry Overall Marketing Plan

Purpose of Marketing Function:

- Differentiate our church/ministry from the competition
- Keep existing members
- Meet and exceed member expectations
- Create new members
- Make our organization the kind of place that people want to do business with
- Operate in an ethical manner
- Monitor the pulse of the marketplace
- Serve and contribute as a member of the organizational team
- Maintain a positive image of the organization with all advertisements

Environmental Factors Specific to Marketing: Market Analysis

1. Member Analysis—How do people in attendance feel about the church/program experience?

2. Competitive Analysis/Benchmarking—What are other organizations doing?

3. Market Research—What you need to know and how to get the information: surveys, focus groups.

General Marketing Strategy

Identify Key Market Segments.

_____

_____

_____

_____

Develop a Marketing Strategy for each market segment. Market research and focus groups should be considered to get specific attitudes and information about each individual group.

1. _____

2. _____

3. _____

4. _____

5. _____

6. _____

What advertising/promotions do you expect to be the best opportunity in the year 2005?

_____
_____
_____

Which promotion/advertising and other marketing strategies will decline and/or present a problem to remain in competition in five years (2009)?

_____
_____
_____

Put yourself in your members' shoes. Why are they coming to your church?

_____
_____
_____

What is your competition doing that could be a threat?

_____
_____
_____

How Do Products/Services/Programs Fit Performance/Potential Matrix?

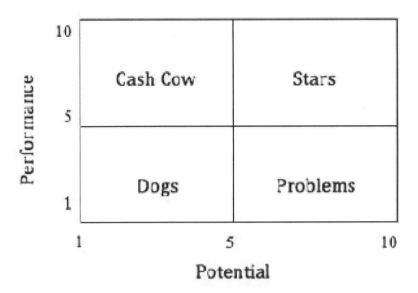

Where do all (or most) of marketing efforts fit product life cycle?

_____

_____

_____

_____

Intro   Growth   Mature   Decline

List Church/Ministry Programs

A. _____

B. _____

C. _____

D. _____

E. _____

Marketing Strengths and Weaknesses

Strengths:

_____

_____

_____

Weaknesses:

_____

_____

_____

Marketing Assumptions

1. _____

2. _____

3. _____

OBJECTIVES

	Last Year Actual	Next Year	5 Years
Total Attendance			
Membership			
Programs			
Organization			
Training			
Development			
Promotion			

MARKETING STRATEGY

What products/services/programs should be added to present product mix?

_____

_____

_____

What products/services/programs should be dropped from present product mix?

_____

_____

_____

How do you react to a rapidly changing market place? What opportunities are available due to changes? What are key marketing strategies?

_____

_____

_____

MONITORING AND CONTROL

1. Performance Analysis

2. Member Data Feedback

MARKETING ACTION PLAN

Objectives: _____

Overall Responsibility:_____

Strategies: _____

Start Date			
Action Steps			
Due Date			
Responsibility			
Status			

SET UP A WAY TO MONITOR HOW YOU ARE DOING AND A WAY TO CREATE ACTION

An action plan for each objective area should be developed. It helps goals come to life with appropriate action.

ACTION PLAN OBJECTIVE:

Action Plan			
Person Responsible			
Date Start			
Date Completed			

STRATEGIES

1. _____

2. _____

3. _____

4. _____

5. _____

SALES MANAGEMENT PLAN

Now that the marketing plan is developed, it is time to develop a sales management plan. Ideally, managers and salesmen have been in on developing the marketing plan. It is important that those who execute the plan are in on the plan. The task is to develop a sales management plan, which in effect executes the marketing plan.

1. Organize sales force.

2. Select sales force.

3. Train sales people.

4. Motivate sales people.

5. Set quotas, goals, objectives for total sales effort down to individual salespersons.

6. Compensation plan that encourages performance.

7. Evaluate progress.

Appendix C:
Strategic Plan: Calvary Temple of Temple Terrace

Purpose

Environmental Analysis

- City of Temple Terrace trying to annex CT & other surrounding properties.
- Attention given to security/morals within clergy & church leadership
- Just a Few Miles Away from Major Center of Financial Terrorist Cell Activity
- Dysfunctional Family Units, Single Parents, Abusive Relationships are at higher levels than ever before — people are searching for relationships.
- High-tech, Low-touch population, Fast food mentality, Desensitized Generation
- Cultural diversity of population—African American and Islamic, etc.
- Calvary Temple is NOT the closest charismatic church to New Tampa— Competition
- Busy families — Busy lives, Area Events (School Sport, etc.) — Negative — Keep youth from being involved.
- Possible war in the Middle East-Area. Small groups will become more important if gas prices rise.
- Area events — Sporting Events, Gasparilla, School functions, College-Expanded USF Football Team.
- Area demographics: New neighborhood housing developments. Student Housing development for College.
- Peer pressure on all age levels
- Population growth—ten miles north & south
- Few people from nearby community attend Calvary Temple.
- Area college growth — New housing & apartment developments for USF & Motels/Hotels for USF Football Team.
- Prime time vacation spot, hotel spots
- MacDill Air Force Base—Central Command Move to Middle East?? Financial Impact.
- Transient population, within Tampa as well as moving in and out of Tampa
- Commuter congregation — Thonotosassa, Lutz, Plant City, etc.
- Post modern era—No absolutes, no boundaries, extreme games
- Increase in transportation and visualization of church.
- Teen parents and grandparents raising their grandchildren.

- Loss in income — Lay offs.

Strengths

- Friendliness & Relationships among members & to new guests.
- Heightened sense of anticipation of members
- Small Group Stabilization
- Great improvement on communication & relationships between Ministry Groups.
- Great improvement on first impressions for visitors and CT members.
- Outreach to youth is improving daily.
- Support from top > down towards all ministry groups
- Youth Ministry & Facility
- High integrity of Finances of church and Finance Committee
- Addition of Information Booth
- Better use of time
- Identified our area of weakness & have acted upon it — Gifting
- Staffed for growth
- Personal contacts with members & shepherding congregation
- New Road — Temple Terrace Highway
- Continued organization, communication, management & strategic planning.
- Church Van Purchased.
- Dynamic Pastor & Wife — Role models, integrity, respect and longevity in ministry — Relative sermon topics.
- Computer system — updated, server bought.
- Small groups Functioning Children's and Youth programs.
- Strong focus on evangelism.
- Debt Free property/facilities
- Corporation longevity.
- Longevity in geographical location.
- Leadership.
- Focus on vision "Every House a Lighthouse, Every Person a Shining Light."
- Positive outlook.
- Family heritage and legacy in the ministry.
- Good accumulation of tangible property
- Functional facilities with space available for growth.

- Organized Greeter/Usher program at front door.
    - Power Point and outline of the sermons.
- Age diversity on the platform.
- Part of the charismatic growth movement.
- Volunteer participation

Weaknesses

- Lack of web presence
- Lack of growth
- Lack of signage
- Marketing — Marketing Plan Needs More Attention from Management Team/ Leadership, Message Board Out Front/Side, Radio, TV, billboards—(See Marketing Plan)
- Working on Formal public commitment to Calvary Temple
- Assimilation
- Ownership of Calvary Temple in general.
- Core group overextended
- Cultural diversity not reflected in our leadership — Need to decide who we are targeting.
- Programs for single dysfunctional families.
- Outreach to the immediate community.
- Inadequate A/C in Life Training Center.
- Interior Sanctuary dated, not as contemporary and appealing as necessary. Not functioning at optimum, technically and visually.
- No college outreach or Jr. High transitioning
- Training plan in place for Pastor Brooks and others in leadership positions
- Sound system and acoustics
- Projection screen distorted.
- Balcony sight line.
- Inefficient flow of information, trickle down effect not working.
- Bookstore — Lack of Leadership
- Audio Ministry — Lack of Leadership

Objectives and Goals

	Last Year's Goal	**Next Year 2003**	**Five Years**	**Status Oct., 2002**
Attendance	350	366	830	305 Avg.
Membership	700	700	1,500	520 Avg.
Building			Youth Building Remodel Sanctuary	Youth/ Children's Rooms Remodeled COMPLETE
Missions	10%	10%	10%	10%
Facilities	Pave Parking Lot	Note projects next page		New Paved Parking Lot **COMPLETE**
Financial	Stay within budget	Increase by 10% Stay within budget	Increase by 10% Stay within budget	Over Budget 10%
People	5 Full time 4 Part time	7 Full time 5 Part time	Training 15 Full time 30 Part time	6 Full Time 5 Part Time

Revised General Strategies

- Continued movement towards complete Small Group structure
- Improve image — Physical update
- Consider construction of new Youth Building
- Continue emphasis on Goals in front of congregation to reach out — Result: Increased Attendance.
- Beginning Membership Classes once per month along with Pastor's Receptions. This will improve new visitor family assimilation. Institute plan to assimilate visitors to active members.
- Small group structure improvement (Interns ready to lead) Inspire and strengthen small leaders with public recognition and perks (retreats, trips, etc.) for goals met. Proper training, commitment, communication and accountability a must for success.

- Survey Calvary Temple's population

- Address volunteer issues — Find Leadership. Restructure entire volunteer program. Will use Red Cross Volunteer Plan as guideline. Possible "Volunteer Boot Camp" w/Barbara Rarden.

- Continue to increase technology — Web-site project. Technology Task Force in place includes, Dan Doidge, Michelle Hawthorne, Craig Brooks, David Durcan & Kerry Rydman

- Develop and organize music, youth and children's department staff — See Key Result Area for children

- Update Music—Music department will begin to use more diversity in music presentation. Perhaps endeavoring to learn more current songs and music as they were written. New music ordered from Hillsongs in Australia and from Clint Brown in Orlando, FL. Britt O'Steen has been placed in leadership position over vocal segment of praise and worship.

  - Prayer and praise reports — Need to be a regular part of Sunday services and Small Group meetings.

- Plan of succession for Pastor Brooks and others in leadership positions — Each person will begin grooming and training a replacement. There should always be three people in consideration for replacement. Consider an organizational strategy utilizing a Small Group Pastor or Associate Pastor.

- David Road & Temple Terrace Highway area — Continue to review and increase community awareness about Calvary.

- Review Marketing strategy — Review Palm Spring Marketing Plan compare it to plan submitted by Dan Doidge. Leadership needed for Committee and members ascertained.

Calvary Temple Administrative and Operational Structure

Purpose: To have clear concise expectations on the administration and operation of Calvary Temple. To communicate to all Ministry Group Leaders the structure and organizational changes that are being implemented and the process to which those changes will be accomplished.

I. Administrative Structure

    A. Corporate Structure of Calvary Temple

        President — Pastor Dale A. Brooks

        Vice President — C.L. Brooks

        Treasurer — Kaye Brooks

        Directors — Bill Morris, Al Werly

B. Eldership of Calvary Temple

Pastor Dale & Mrs. Kaye Brooks

Mr. & Mrs. C.L. Brooks

Dr. & Mrs. Peter Knight

Mr. & Mrs. Bill Morris

C. Ministry Group Leadership

Ministry Group Administrator — Pastor Brooks

Operations Administrator — Michelle Hawthorne

Visitation/Member — Erlene Rowland

Finance — Bill Morris

Youth — Erik Ronne

Children's — Zana Brooks

Music — Kent Smith

Facilities Maintenance — John Parks

Ushers — Gregg Mayer

Greeters — Dennis Piller

Marketing —

Audio Visual —

D. Small Group Leadership

Small Group Administrator-Scott Bartlett

Small Group Administrative Assistant-Angela Bartlett

Zone Leaders–Jim & Jeri McCance, Jack & Linda Gross, Dennis & Dyan Piller, and C.L. & Cynthia Brooks

II.   Operational Structure

Administrative/Operational Meetings

Meeting	Attendees	Timeframe
Management Team	Pastor Brooks meets w/ SG Admin. Youth & Children's Ldrs & their Assistants	Monthly-Second Tuesday 6:30-7:30 pm

Finance Committee	Pastor meets w/Finance Committee	Weekly-Tuesday 8:00 am
Church Staff	Pastor meets w/ All Office Staff	Weekly-Tuesday 8:30-9:30 am
3-2-1 Planning	Pastor Brooks meets w/ Music, Children Leaders, & Admin. Asst.	Every Week-Tuesday 9:30-10:30 am
Ministry Group Leaders	Pastor meets w/ Ministry Group Leaders & Admin. Asst.	Monthly-Second Tuesday 7:30-9:00 pm
All Small Group Leaders	Small Group Administrator meets w/ All Small Group Leaders & Zone Leaders	Monthly-First & Third Sunday 12:00 noon
Zone Leaders	Zone Leaders meet w/ Small Group Administrators	Monthly-Third Tuesday 7:00-9:00 pm

III. Contents Of Terms

Term	Description
Sunday Large Group gatherings: 8 am and 10	Sunday morning corporate gatherings-8 am and 10 am services.
Ministry Group Leaders	Former Department Heads-Example: Music Dept.
Small Groups	Former cell groups-interest based/sermon groups
Zone Leaders	Former Zone Pastors-usually consists of five or more Section Leaders or small group leaders
Section Leaders	Consists of five or more small groups.
Small Group Leaders	Former Cell groups.

Appendix D:
Strategic Plan: Inner City Marketing Plan

(Wyketia Washington created this strategic plan as part of a class project for a Langston University masters class in 2012.)

Strategic Objective

The purpose of this plan is to document tactical information for Grace Missionary Community Church (GMCC), and to identify opportunities for a long-term relationship with the Southside neighborhood within a 2 mile radius of 73129 zip code to increase membership and community program opportunities.

GMCC Background

Church Profile

GMCC is a non-denominational religious organization whose mission is to win souls to Christ one at a time through prayer, teaching, preaching, living and faith.

Church Purpose

To spiritually equip souls with the tools of accepting salvation, understanding: grace, mercy, love and peace in preparation of evangelizing to others within the community, city, state, nation, and world-wide

Church Vision

To become a dedicated and committed multicultural body of believers

Environmental Analysis

- Few people from nearby community attend Grace Missionary Community Church
- Dysfunctional Family Units, Single Parents, Abusive Relationships, Homelessness, Drug & Alcohol Abuse are at higher levels than ever before—people are searching for relationships
- Cultural diversity of current GMCC population:
  - African
  - African American

Church Organization Chart

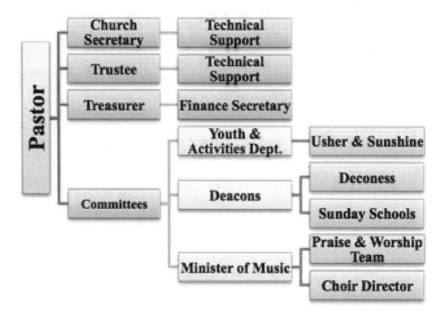

Strengths

- Debt free property/facilities
- Great location
- Web presence
- Sound system & acoustics

Weaknesses

- Lack of growth
- Lack of signage
- Lack of strategic plan
- Lack of marketing plan
- Core group overextended
- No college outreach or Young Adult Programs
- Inefficient flow of information—trickledown effect not working

Objectives & Goals

	2011	2012	2013	2014	2015
Attendance	n/a	50	100	150	200

Membership	15	21	29	44	66
Growth	0%	40%	40%	50%	50%
Facilities	Phase 1: Parking lot	Phase 2: Parking lot	Remodel Phase 1	Remodel Phase 2	Remodel Phase 3
Financial	Stay within budget	Increase by 10% Stay within budget	Increase by 10% Stay within budget	Increase by 10% Stay within budget	Increase by 10% Stay within budget

Administrative & Operational Structure

To have a clear vision of Grace Missionary Community Church and to better serve its members this section provides an overview of organizational formation.

I.   Administrative Structure

A.   Corporate Structure of Grace Missionary Community Church

- President—Pastor Tabe W. Brownell
- Vice President—Vacant
- Treasure—Celestine Watkins
- Secretary—LaVon Clark
- Financial Secretary—Julius Karnwie
- Chair Advisory Committee—Francis Williams

B.   Eldership of Grace Missionary Community Church

- Pastor Tabe W. Brownell

C.   2012 Officers for Grace Missionary Community Church

- Director of Christian Education—Evang. Roland Pannah
- Minister of Music—Vacant
- Choir Leader—Biakardor Johnson
- Director of Ushers—Vacant
- Director of Youth—Josephine Pannah
- Pastor's Armor Bearer—Margret Jackson

II.   Operational Structure

Administrative/Operational Meetings

Meeting	Attendees	Timeframe
Church Staff	Pastor meets w/ all staff	2nd Saturday @ 11am
Church Officers	Pastor meets w/ all officers	Month of April & October
General Church	Pastor meets w/ all members	Month of July & December
Committee	Pastor meets w/ committees:	
	Church Anniversary	Month of February
	Pastor's Anniversary	Month of August

Marketing Plan

Purpose of Marketing Function

- Differentiate GMCC organization and services from competition
- Keep existing members
- Meet and exceed members expectations
- New member invitation
- Make GMCC the kind of organization that people want to business with
- Operate in an ethical manner
- Serve and contribute to community
- Maintain a positive image

Environmental Dynamics Specific to GMCC

While researching and composing these market analysis considerations of uncontrollable factors were acknowledged.

I.   Customer Analysis

Capturing a glimpse outlook of this organization was accomplished through the usage of online survey delivered via email. The responders are actual individuals who have at some point attended or are attending Grace Missionary Community Church. The survey consisted of ten questions upon which four are listed below.

If a new community program or order of service were available, how likely would you be to attend our church instead of another church service currently available from other churches?

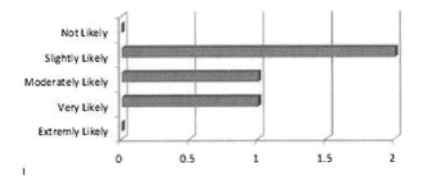

|

How important is convenience when choosing this type of service?

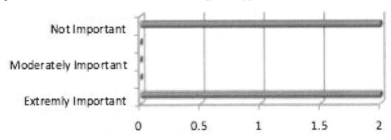

Overall, are you satisfied with your experience at GMCC?

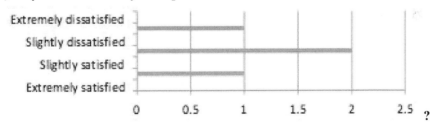

?

If community services were available today, how likely would you be to recommend it to others?

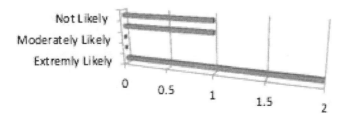

II.   Competitive Analysis

There are approximately 22 churches in the 73129 zip code area. In this area there are: (10) Baptist Churches, (3) Pentecostal Churches, (2) Methodist churches, and (4) churches were the denomination is unknown.

Chart 1
Information retrieved on 03/28/12 from
www.indexedamerica.com

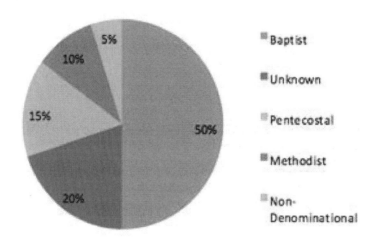

Out of the twenty-two churches within the area only two of these religious organizations have websites; Grace Missionary Community Church and one other.

III.   Market Research

Charity, Civics & Religious 501 C-3 Nonprofit organizations within 73129 zip code area:

Charity—(5) Informational, (1) Local/Regional, (7) National

Civic—(11) Organizations

Social Services—(2) Organizations

Religious—(22) Churches

Figure 1. Demographic Quick Facts from the Nielsen Company.
2012 Population by Single Classification Race

Native Hawaiian and Other
Asian Alone
Black or African American Alone
Two or More Races
American Indian and Alaska
Some Other Race Alone
Not Hispanic or Latino
Hispanic or Latino
0
10000
20000
30000
40000
Household Income 1 mile
Household Income 2 miles
1 Mile Radius
2 Mile Radius

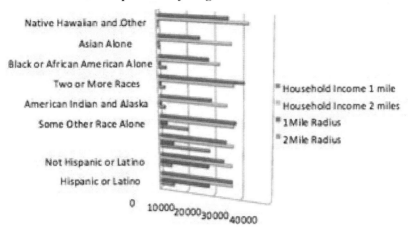

Figure 2. Household Quick Facts
2012 Report from the Nielsen Company

2012 Houshold Type for 73129
1 Mile Radius (Pop. 1931)
2 Mile Radius (Pop. 7905)
Male Householder, no own children
Male Householder, own children
Female Householder, no own children
Female Householder, own children
Married-Couple Family, own children
Married-Couple Family, no own children
118
511
210
625
194
370
892
477
1558
2052
561
2267

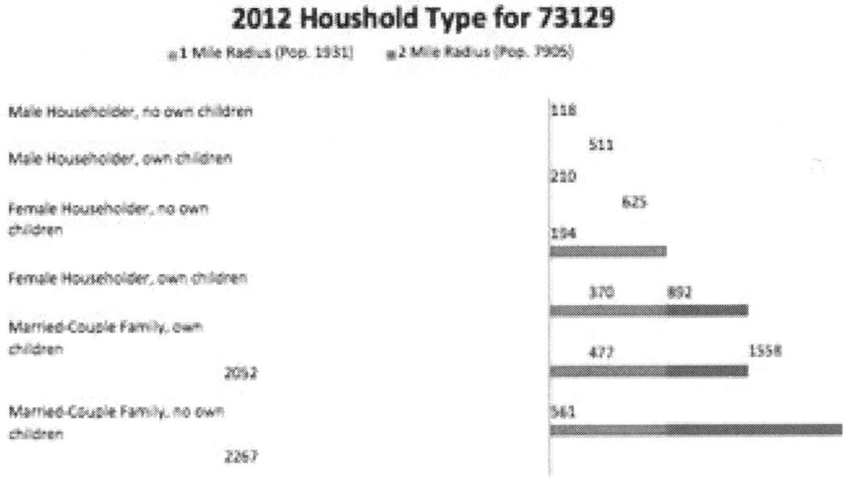

Figure 3. Population Quick Facts
2012 Report by the Nielsen Company

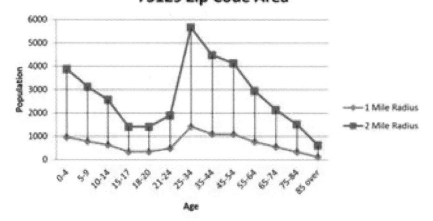

Figure 4. Data taken from 2005 U.S. Dept. of Education
National Center for Education Studies

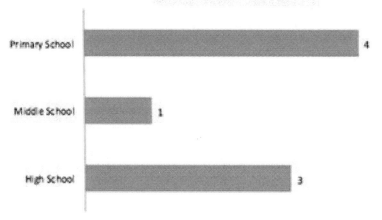

Figures 5-8.
Detailed Profile from Onboard Informatics
www.city-data.com

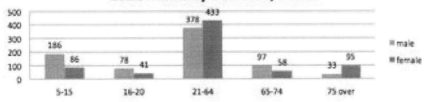

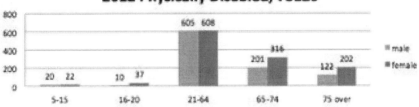

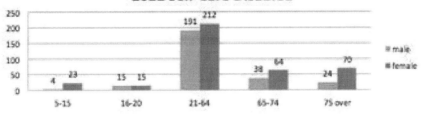

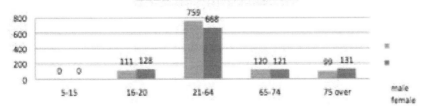

Key Market Segments

A. Churches in 73129 zip code area

B. Hispanic, Latino, and White people

C. Married Coupled people with & without children, and Female Householder with children

D. Ages 25-54

E. High School Kids

F. Disabled

The best products and or services that I foresee in 2012-2013 are:

1. Creating a network of resources by developing an alliance with local churches.

2. Establishing life coaching and literacy programs that teaches reading and English as a second language.

3. Provide counseling services: Marriage and Spiritual Guidance.

4. Make available community recreational activities that engages and promote family unity

All of the above mentioned ideas are resilient and increases the likelihood of durability while presenting the opportunity for job creation and eventually self-sufficiency.

The Grace Missionary Community Church site is a perfect location to execute strategically.

The 2 mile radius surrounding the grounds of GMCC is in such dire need that any competition does not pose a threat.

Marketing Strengths

*   Greater attendee satisfaction
*   Increased attendee participation
*   Better attraction of market resources
*   Greater efficiency

Marketing Weakness

*   Need for volunteers and experienced workers
*   Danger that GMCC's social responsibility actions may add cost, reduced focus on core business, and possibly alienate some persons

- Discovering niche to attract Hispanic, Latino, and Whites

Marketing Objectives

Total Contributions

Last Year Actual	Next Year	5 Years
$13,330.51	$21,0001	$999,225

- To deliver and promote low-to-no-cost programs of needed services
- To offer a worship service with sermon and readings geared to working adults every Wednesday night, to be followed by coffee and dessert in the social hall. This will be highlighted in the church bulletin and listed in the "worship section" on our website.
- To introduce a regular column in the church bulletin geared to the problems of working adults.
- To develop a church bowling team for adult couples during winter months and recruit through the church bulletin and community newspapers. Twelve couples should participate the first year.
- To facilitate the organization of adult groups to work in other existing social programs at given times. For example, Monday will become GMCC's night at the community clothes closet. By the end of the year more than 100 people should be participating in these groups. Announcements of this activity will be made regularly at the pulpit, listed on website and included in church e-blasts.

Financial Forecast

The purpose of this financial plan is to raise $105,000 to establish a community based program for the 73129 zip code area.

The Environmental Factors Specific to Finance

The proposed budget of $105,000 will be raised by organizing a benefits/ Award Dinner.

Financial Strength

- Money will be used to aid marketing objectives.
- Event will benefit all involved.
- Money will be cycled through local businesses working homogeneously. Right timing increases participation and funding.

EVENT INCOME AND EXPENSES
(Donor Benefit with Honoree)

INCOME		EXPENSE	
Corporate Sponsors		Crab Cards	$831
4 @ $10,000	$40,000	Dinner / Reception	$33,321
9 @ $5,000	$45,000	Flowers	$3,025
8 @ $3,000	$24,000	Invitation—Design & Printing	$3,609
18 @ $2,000	$36,000	Piano	$100
Ticket Sales		Postage	$726
90 @ $200	$18,000	Program Design & Printing	$3,446
Total Income	$163,000	Save the Date Postcards—Printing	$639
		Save the Date Postcards—Design	$1,040
		Vellum Paper for Invitation & Program	$716
		Video Equipment	$1,628
		Video Production	$7,740
		Voice-over	$1,500
		Total Expenses	$58,375
		NET INCOME	$104,625

Financial Weakness

- Funds needed for initial event start-up campaign
- Cost reported covers direct expenses only; not included an allocation for staff for overload
- Staffs for event overhead costs are contingent upon timing and proposal placement.

Total Revenue

Next Year	5 Years
$163,000	1,000,000

Some Return on Investment and/or Equity

Next Year	5 Years
$105,000	$640,000

Major Financial Objectives

- To adequately fund program to increase probability of efficiency
- To ensure a reasonable balance of program outflow & inflows maintaining stability.
- To invest in areas of need that are conducive to family structure, community growth, unity, and peace.
- To reduce uncertainties with regards to life change.

Income Statement	This Year	Year 1	Year 2	Year 3	Year 4	Year 5
		163,000	228,200	342,300	513,450	770,175
Revenue	15,000	21,000	29,400	44,100	66,150	99,225
Tithes & Offering	15,000					
Cost of Goods Sold: Love Offering: Pastor's Salary	700	8,400	11,760	17,640	26,460	39,690
Love Offering: Worship Leader		3,900		7,800	7,800	7,800
Love Offering: Children's Ministry Leader		2,600		7,800	31,200	13,000
Love Offering: Musicians		5,200	5,200	7,800	10,400	13,000
Love Offering: Church Secretary		5,200	7,280	10,920	16,380	24,570
Total Cost of Goods Sold	700	25,300	37,240	51,960	92,240	98,060

Gross Margin	14,300	158,701	220,362	334,443	487,364	771,345
Gross Margin Percentage	95%	86%	86%	87%	84%	89%
Utilities	2,788	2,927	3,074	3,227	3,389	3,558
Security Alarm	496	496	496	496	496	496
Building Insurance	700	700	700	700	700	700
Event Expense		58,375	58,375	58,375	58,375	58,375
Postage		3,600	3,600	3,600	3,600	3,600
Outreach Program	734	734	734	734	734	734
Guest Speaker	100	100	100	100	100	100
Equipment		10,000	8,000	6,000		
Remodeling Church			50,000	25,000	10,000	
Total Expense	4,818	76,933	125,079	98,233	77,394	67,563
GMCC-Operating Income	9,482	81,768	95,283	236,210	40,970	703,782
Depreciation		(2,000)	(4,000)	(6,000)	(6,000)	(6,000)
Other Income		3,000	4,200	6,300	9,450	14,175
Net Income Before Tax	9,482	82,768	95,483	236,510	413,420	711,957
Taxes (assume 8.75%)	9,482	375	525	786	1181	1772
Net Income After Taxes	9,482	82,393	94,958	235,723	412,239	710,185
Add Back Depreciation		2,000	4,000	6,000	6,000	6,000
Cash Flow	9,482	84,393	98,958	241,723	418,239	716,185
Present Value		75,351	78,889	172,054	265,798	406,382

Sum of Present Value of Future Cash Flows	$998,474
Alternate Net Present Value	$1,007,956

Human Resources Plan

Grace Missionary Community Church has two filled volunteer positions:

- **Pastor** — In the upcoming year this position will be issued a love offering of $161 per week and will incur an annual 40% increase during years 1-2; and an 50% increase thus after.

- **Church Secretary** — In the upcoming year this position will be issued a love offering of $100 per week and will incur and annual 40% increase during years 1-2; and an $50% increase thus after.

GMCC will be soliciting for volunteer staff to fill the following vacant positions over the following course of time.

POSITIONS	YR 1	YR 2	YR 3	YR 4	YR 5	Wkly Love Offering
Minister of Music	1	2	2	2	2	Each @ $75
Children's Ministry Leader	1	2	3	4	5	Each @ $50
Musicians	2	2	3	4	5	Each @ $50
Internships	Varies	Varies	Varies	Varies	Varies	Under construction

**Some volunteered positions will convert to employment contingent upon membership increasing and maintained beyond 100 and/or GMCC's operating income exceeds $150k.

Recruitment/Selection

The searching process will be to meet with as many interested volunteers as possible through utilizing three main avenues:

1. Asking others — friends, churches, colleges, religious outlets, etc.

2. Attending Worship Conferences

3. On-line searches

Incentives

Minister of Music — Will be allowed to organize fundraising musical concerts having access to all church property, equipment and marketing materials. Profits from events shall be divided accordingly.

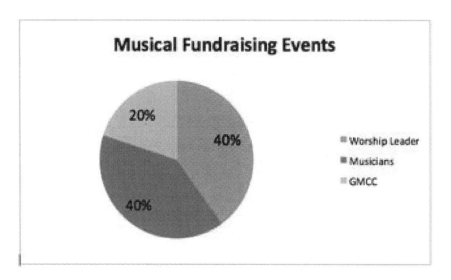

Benefits

After two calendar year of rendered services volunteers are afforded a complementary 2 night stay in a suite at La Quinta Inn along with a dinner for two and movie.

Training & Development

It is important for volunteer staff stay abreast of updated ministry offerings. GMCC will provide access to

• Online webinars

• Management training

• Safety and Heath Seminars

Children's Ministry Leaders

Will be allowed to organize fundraising productions (via plays, etc) having access to all church property, equipment and marketing materials. Profits from events shall be divided accordingly.

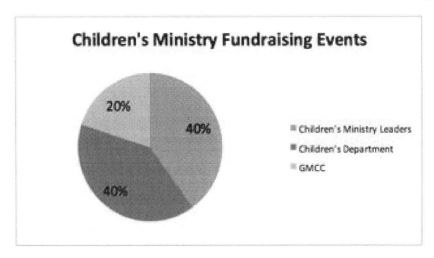

Benefits

After two calendar year of rendered services volunteers are afforded a complementary 2 night stay in a suite at La Quinta Inn along with a dinner for two and movie.

Training & Development

It is important for volunteer staff stay abreast of updated ministry offerings. GMCC will provide access to

- Online webinars
- Management training
- Safety and Heath Seminars

Performance Appraisals

- Evaluations of performances will be conducted twice a year
- Evaluations will be based upon job description o How well were specific goals reached—Evaluations will be used to justify salary

Action Plan

- Attract Membership from Hispanics, Latinos, and Whites
- Re-build Church's Operational System
- Create Networks of Resources with local Churches
- Create Life Coaching & Literacy Program teaching English as a second language and visa versa
- Provide Counseling Services: Pre, Existing, Post Couples/Marriage Therapy and Spiritual Guidance.
- Create Recreational Activities that are family friendly

Appendix E
Planning, Organization, and Common Sense
Leadership with a Biblical Perspective

Case Study
Things Got Out of Whack at the Church

Ken Brasfield was a computer design specialist. He was busy working on the final stages of the installation of a sophisticated computerized system for the church. Frank Roma, Church Business Manager, was in charge of the overall project. Roma had negotiated a deadline for installation which was ten days away. The sales contract provided for a severe price penalty in case the church wasn't ready. The church had to have their part of the job done when the company delivered the equipment and brought its service personnel into town.

The Senior Pastor, Jim Jones, had been there 18 months. He was easy going, loved to do public relations work and stay in touch with the congregation, visit hospitals and lead prayer groups. He ignored the business of church. He stayed clear of any strife or problem-solving.

Ken Brasfield's immediate boss was Chuck Creekmore, an associate pastor. Roma also reported to Creekmore. Last night, Ken Brasfield phoned Mr. Creekmore and told him that he was quitting immediately. He had all he could take from Roma, and he had decided to leave the church as an employee immediately. Ken told Mr. Creekmore that Roma had been "breathing down his neck" continuously and pressuring him needlessly to get the job completed. Ken assured Mr. Creekmore that he had been doing his best but that in a sophisticated installation of this sort, many things create problems and interfere with getting quick results. Ken said that he didn't attempt to explain the problems to Roma because in Ken's words, "Roma knows next to nothing about the intricate nature of the problems involved." The "straw that broke his back" was a threat from Roma to lock him in the building until the installation was operable even if he had to bring him his food. Ken said he realized that Roma did not intend to do this, but saying this after everything else he had done was too much to take. In Brasfield's view, Roma was a Theory Triple X Manager all the way!

Mr. Creekmore wondered what to do. Mr. Creekmore knew that people with Ken's skills were hard to find. Particularly at this stage of the project, it would be next to impossible to get a replacement employee who could come in to pick up the installation where Ken Brasfield had left off and complete the projection time. Mr. Creekmore understood the meaning of a penalty for late delivery.

The next morning, Associate Pastor Creekmore decided to meet with Frank Roma, Church Business Manager, to discuss the situation.

1.   What are the major and minor problems?

2.   Analyze the case.

3.   Develop alternative solutions. What are the pros and cons of each alternative?

4.   Which alternative is best?

5.   What should Brasfield have done at the beginning of the assignment?

6.   If you were Roma's boss, what would you do?

7.   How could this situation have been avoided in the first place?

Care and Feeding of the Boss Care

Everyone in the beginning literally with birth, develops a continuing series of relationships with other persons. Without realizing it, we develop relationships with parents, siblings and other relatives.

As we grow older we learn to deal with teachers, counselors, athletic coaches and pastors. Later comes college, and some of us even become skilled in the gamesmanship between ourselves and the faculty. Some of us have even had the rare opportunity to get to know a drill sergeant in the military.

Eventually most of us, for which society is grateful, go to work and begin paying taxes. That's when we cease to live off the system and become a contributing part. That's when the game of life takes some dramatic changes. At this point we develop a brand new and most vital relationship—that with our new boss.

Every person faces this challenge. Every person, even if they have been on the job for a period of time still faces the same challenges.

This new boss is a person, too, and has gone through the same stages that we have. The difference, and it's a big difference, is that he is one step ahead of us. He has power, the ability to reward and punish, both openly and subtly.

Because of this, we tend to assume that this formidable person has the keen insight to manage us properly. Some of us fail to realize that while we are learning how to deal with him he also has a boss to contend with, and the problems associated with that relationship.

As I have managed through a wide range of positions in industry and academia, and consulted and advised in a wide range of organizations, I have had the opportunity to study this process, both as player and as interested onlooker.

I have noted that the state of uncertainty by all players in the game as to where they stand in the organization is a common denominator that treads through this entire process. This is accompanied by a fair degree of anxiety and apprehension as to what is expected of one by higher management levels and whether one is meeting those expectations.

I believe it is important to recognize this as a natural process, and that steps should be taken to cope. If these steps relieve the uncertainty, performance might be improved.

For starters, I propose the following steps:

1. Ask your boss to develop a list of five key, specific, measurable results he wants you to accomplish over the next year.

2. Simultaneously, develop a similar list for yourself—what you believe you should accomplish during the next year.

3. Meet and discuss your lists. Be prepared for some disagreement between them.

4. Reach agreement on what you're to accomplish. Knowing what's expected of you will give you direction and thus increase your sense of security.

5. Now get with it, making sure you manage your resources well to assure the results.

6. Keep your boss informed on your progress; he does not like surprises.

7. At year end, review the year; see where you stand and then start the process over again.

What most employees fail to understand is that it is their primary responsibility to make sure their boss is successful—to help prevent his making a mistake.

You can be sure your boss wants to be successful. He has you on the team to help ensure that success. If he has any reason to suspect you of disloyalty or of failure to work for the common good, you're in trouble. The seven steps listed above help you assure the boss you are on target with his expectations.

It's also important to recognize that it is his perception of your contribution that is of prime importance, and not necessarily your perception. With this in mind, isn't it a good idea to find out from him exactly what results he expects?

As you study ways and means to "care for and feed your boss,"—be sure that you honor and respect the responsibility he/she has. Make sure you are loyal to the cause and are making a contribution.

1. What is the purpose of your job?

2. What are your key measurable objectives?

Individual Planning Seminar Worksheet

1. Describe the vision and dream you have for your life.

   How would you describe yourself to someone you have never seen?
   Would your friends describe you the same way?
   List the three people who have had the greatest influence on your life.
   What was the major influence from each?
   List your favorite social activities and hobbies.
   List three things that have made you feel good this month.
   Write out a one-paragraph description of the purpose of your life.
   List three things you like to do.
   List three things you do not like to do.

2. What's going on in the world around you?

3. What are your strengths?

4. What are your weaknesses?

   List some failures.
   Are these failures holding you back?

5. Rank your job goals from 1st to 8th.

   1. _____ Boss's expectations

   2. _____ Prestige and status

   3. _____ Job security

   4. _____ Opportunity for independent thought and action

   5. _____ Higher salary, more benefits, or both

   6. _____ Recognition for good performance

   7. _____ Promotion to a better job

   8. _____ Personal growth and development

   What do you like about your job?
   What do you feel needs improving on your job?
   How much of your potential do you feel you are achieving?

6. Write a one-paragraph description of how you want your life to be in five years.

7. Write a one-paragraph description of how you want your life to be in one year.

8. For the following categories, what and where do you want to be:

   Next Year
   In Five Years?

   1. Spiritually

   2. Career, Position

   3. Family

   4. Health : Weight, Exercise

   5. Financial: Income, Net Worth

   6. Entertainment: Fun/Hobbies/Vacation

   7. Other

9. How will you get there?

10. What are four things you must do in the next five months to get where you want to be next year and in five years?

11. What are four things holding you back?

12. How do you overcome each of the four obstacles listed above?

13. Whose help do you need to achieve your potential and get where you want to be in five years?

14. Take an objective and use this worksheet to turn it into action.

    Objective: (make it specific, measurable and within a time frame)
    Strategy: (your game plan to achieve each objective)
    Action Plan: (what are steps needed, when to start, what to do — cut goals down to small bites)

15. Who can you discuss your plan with?

    What will happen when you discuss your plan?
    Can they help monitor your progress?

16. Reward yourself for accomplishment!!!

How Big: A Plan or Accident?

How should the church/ministry grow and expand? The central question is whether to grow wildly or control growth. Another question has to do with size of the church/ministry in the long run. Or maybe it's time to retrench. When you grow at will you are reacting to opportunity. This was the strategy of General Patton in World War II: "Take as much ground every day as you can." For the church, it's expand your market as fast as possible. The notion is "big is better." Many believe the opportunity is there, and you better not pass it by or perhaps it will be gone forever.

Should the church ministry grow and expand? While the answer to that question may seem obvious, it is not as clear as it might seem. While we suggest that the church should grow, growth does not always mean expansion. In addition to getting larger, growth may mean getting smaller, better, or simply changing into something different. To make the choice as to how to grow and how much, it is necessary to understand why churches/ministries should grow in the first place.

Why Should Churches/Ministries Grow?

To answer the question—why should churches/ministries grow—we must understand how organizations grow as systems. We start with the presumption that any organization is a system. We know that all systems by nature may self-destruct in a process theorists call entropy. Entropy is the tendency for an organized system to become disorganized—essentially to fall apart. We can explain the tendency toward falling apart by borrowing liberally from Newton's laws and applying them to the church setting.

Church revitalization expert, Norman Shawchuck, observes the church as any other organizational system: a set of interrelated elements within a particular environment. Constituting its nature and mission are certain subsystems that are crucial to its existence: its organizational structure, human relational system, and theological or belief structure. In order for the church to grow and be healthy, the internal systems must be developed and managed to support that growth. It is here that Newton's laws, as applied to organizations, are helpful in determining how growth can be properly managed for the overall success of the organization.

First Law of Organizations: A Church/Ministry at Rest Tends to Stay at Rest.

We know that organizations don't like to change, that inactivity breeds inactivity and finally complacency. This complacency takes the form of the organizational "couch potato"—the church/ministry that has a routine from which it does not want to detour. However, in the rapidly changing world of today's environment, complacency can spell trouble, as we see from the second law.

Second Law of Organizations: Churches/Ministries at Rest Tend to Decay (or at Least Get Into Trouble).

There is an old saying that goes something like "if you snooze, you lose!" While there is much to recommend stability, the religious world is not a particularly stable place. As a result, complacency means that the church/ministry falls behind. In our world, change occurs at ever-increasing rates. The complacent ministry falls behind even more rapidly. For example, it is impossible for the church to stand still and maintain stability. Attrition alone makes it absolutely necessary to sustain an aggressive proactive approach to outreach.

The typical church must add at least 10 percent new members each year just to offset normal loss. In some volatile environments with a highly transient population, this may run 40% or more. Because people move, die, change churches, and leave for various reasons, the church is always in danger of decline from a leadership that simply does nothing. When you think of how many visitors a church has to attract, win over, induct, and integrate to establish membership, the challenge becomes clearer.

Third Law of Organizations: Churches/Ministries in Trouble Tend to Get Worse!

In his research on bankruptcy, Don Hambrick of Columbia University coined the term "flailing about" to describe the death throes of an organization. When churches/ministries decline, panic often sets in so pastors/evangelists start doing anything they can—as long as they are doing something. Hambrick suggests they flail about looking for a solution. As leaders get increasingly desperate, they also get increasingly poor at making choices, creating a spiral of decline.

Shawchuck describes the failure syndrome in the life of the typical church as beginning with generalized conditions of apathy and an increasingly complacent and reactive posture. In this state, it only takes one crisis of moderate proportions to send what looks like a fairly stable church into a tailspin. The crisis could be set off by a financial setback, a leadership problem, an unforeseen change in the environment, or any number of other influences that would seem manageable under normal circumstances. The result is a deadly cycle of reactions, hasty decisions, and ineffective damage control. This free-fall continues as the church finds it lacks the spiritual and emotional reserves to tackle the problem head-on. Problems increase and multiply until the church is paralyzed by a sense of helplessness. One has no idea of how many dominoes are waiting in place until the first one falls.

Church leaders facing this cycle of increasing dysfunction find that if the internal systems of the church are weak or nonexistent, there is little strength in place to resist the trend. Here the value of organizational strengths becomes evident. The internal systems of good organizational structure, sound policies and procedures, ongoing evaluation, and quality control are essential.

How Does the Church/Ministry Combat the Forces of the Three Laws?

Beating the inevitable decline described above simply requires planned growth. In our terms, growth means on-going development of the organization and its capacity. However, growth, as we indicated previously, does not always mean expansion. Growth can mean getting better.

The church must always be about the work of strengthening the internal systems that make it healthy and able to support ongoing growth. These internal systems include the organizational structure which provides for delegation of responsibility and accountability, the relational system which provides for communication, problem solving, and conflict management, and the theological system or belief structure which provides the church with the philosophy and ideology necessary to support its Christian mission purpose.

Growth may mean a different direction. The Mother's March of Dimes started out to fight polio. In 1957, the organization helped Drs. Salk and Sabin defeat polio for good.

Instead of accepting victory and disbanding, the organization took stock of itself, realized the potential good this effective group could do, and took on a new challenge. The new focus, birth defects, sadly is one that the organization will have reason to battle forever.

Describing how churches/ministries get better or different is beyond the scope of this article. What we can discuss is growth in size. To most people, the growth of a church means getting bigger. We see countless examples of churches and ministries which are growing in numbers but are doing little to grow in corporate strength. On the ministry level we see crowds increasing but little being done to nurture the individual or family to health and wholeness.

However, not all size decisions mean the church/ministry is getting bigger. Sometimes the leaner size can be very effective. As an example, in our neighborhood of Tulsa, one church had successfully addressed the issue of responsible growth with a well-publicized slogan. Dr. James Buskirk of First United Methodist Church wanted people to know that the importance of the individual and the quality of community were a priority in a climate of mega-churches where individuals tended to feel lost and alienated. The slogan: "We don't think bigger is better, we think better is bigger."

Church expert, Carl Dudley, observes that the small church is bigger than the large church in two critical areas: relationships and accountability. He contends that small churches by nature are far better at providing the family atmosphere and personal touch so necessary to the nurture and development of the individual and community. Compared to the Sunday "mega-crowd" where anonymity is the order of service, the small church requires that the individuals involve themselves to know each other and build relationships for the church's survival. Because of this strong interpersonal factor in the small church, such ministries as pastoral care, discipleship, lay-leader training, and fellowship tend to be stronger.

The central question for pastors/evangelists is one of how big the church/ministry should be for the long run. Ralph Moore, one of the new generation's leaders in the cell-group approach to church growth, uses a proactive method of multiplying and managing groups as the primary thrust of evangelism. Instead of adding groups to meet the needs of the growing crowd, he uses the cultivation of healthy cell groups as the primary focus outreach. Based on his experience with Hope Chapel and its 80-plus member churches, he trains pastors in a very direct process of church growth through establishing, building, and reproducing groups. His method is to set up groups with assistant leaders, then to multiply the group by using these assistants and members of existing groups to start new groups in a well-planned cycle. This approach keeps the basic unit of the church and all its nurturing elements intact as the church develops. As a strategy, this approach seems to have unlimited potential for keeping the balance between growth and nurture.

One needs to look no further than the largest church in the world to see this methodology maximized. Dr. Cho built his church in Korea on the concept of a cell for every member. Training lay-leaders and multiplying groups and organizing these groups into networks overseen by capable pastors is the demonstrated dynamic which has challenged traditional approaches to church growth based on the Sunday gathering.

The argument for controlled growth is to be conservatively aggressive. Controlled growth requires more analysis. It is proactive not reactive. In this scenario, the opportunity is minimized for costly mistakes.

Peter Drucker, noted business consultant and author, (1,641) believes a firm has an optimum size in every industry. It is a good theory, but how does the firm determine size? We believe the church/ministry also has an optimum size.

In order for churches to respond to the call for growth, each area of the ministry must have resources. As such, we need to understand the role that resources play. Webster's defines a resource as "something that lies ready for use or can be drawn upon for aid." Traditionally, economists have classified organizational resources into three general categories—land, labor, and capital. However, as we will discuss below, several intangible resources are also essential for firm survival.

While having resources is necessary for growth, just having resources is not sufficient. Churches and ministries can be in the midst of plenty only to die.

Another way to view long-term success of the churches/ministries is with the formula:

$$X = f(a,b,c,d,e, \ldots ?)$$

The (X) represents the dependent variable, long-term success. In the formula, X is function of the various combinations of independent variable, a,b,c,d,e, on to infinity. The discussion could be expanded to independent variables: environment, organization, human relations, theological system, etc.

For example, in the best-case scenario, long-term success (X) of the church could be a function of balancing or adjusting the internal systems of the church to support the numeric growth of the church. Other independent church variables are leadership and specific programs of evangelism, discipleship, and education; these and other independent variables should be integrated.

Conclusion

Our recommendation is a thoughtful, creative approach to strategic planning. The strategic plan is developed by taking all factors into consideration. This process forces the size decision. The options could be to double in size, have modest growth, or as we have seen in the past decades—downsize. The emphasis here is proactive planning. Too often, for example, downsizing is in small increments. It is like cutting the dog's tail one segment at a time. Every cut is painful. A better approach is proactive retrenching and then an aggressive scaled-back attack plan.

Too often a ministry with uncontrolled growth ends up with disillusioned leaders, harassed pastors and staff, confusion, and a declining quality of all programs. It can be likened to an army out-running its fuel and food. The excitement of the rapid advance is sobering as the church/ministry (and the army) becomes vulnerable to attack while mired in their self-imposed quicksand.

When Does the Holy Spirit Take Over and Strategy End?

Introduction

A number of instances involving efforts for church/ministry growth over the years seem to defy ordinary reason. Strategy planning has been used as a tool to develop and expand churches and religious nonprofit organizations. We have both observed two definite instances of what seem to be extraordinary occurrences that have given two churches the opportunity to expand to meet their purpose/mission/ vision. Examples of the intermingling of strategy and Spirit indicate there is another less understood dimension to decision making.

First Example

Members of a church in the Southwest began praying for a valuable piece of property adjacent to the church's small facility. The price was $198,000, ten times what could be afforded. As prayer increased, vision grew. After a year or so, the petition, forged by the Spirit through many months of corporate prayer, became deeper, more meaningful, and very specific: "Father, provide this property for the future outreach of the church; either give us the resources to buy it, or bring the price down so we can afford it." It all came together one cold January morning when the council ventured out of the warm building onto the frosted desert and marched around the property, jumping over humps and tumbleweeds in the Name of the Lord. One of the elders led the charge. After that prayer, they knew something was about to happen.

The chain of events that followed directly related to the prayer that had continued each step of the way without any knowledge of what might eventually come about. The congregation measured developments by the prayer meeting as the plan unfolded from prayer meeting to prayer meeting.

Forgive the detail, but it is the only way you can get the picture of what really happened. First, the city decided to take a four-foot strip off the front of the church property to widen the road. The settlement was $2,400 for the land and after lengthy negotiations the assessor awarded $45,000 for damages. Hence $47,000 was placed in their hands from a totally unexpected source.

Several months later the city took over the expensive property the church was praying for and reappraised it for $38,000 because it had become landlocked from the same road-widening project. The city offered the property to the church for the adjusted price of $38,000. The congregation paid cash with the money the city had recently given them.

After purchasing the land, the bank evaluated the property and said the value went back up to $154,000 because, by becoming joined to their existing parcel, it was no longer landlocked.

Consider the facts: The original owner got his price from the city. The city paid the church for a tiny strip of land the church did not need. The amount the church received was enough to pay for the adjusted price of the land they needed. The value of the land jumped back up in value because it was no longer landlocked. The attorney, who was a member of the church council and watched the whole thing happen said, "Deals like this just don't happen in real estate. Nobody is smart enough to put all this together. It had to have been the prayer!"

After the two years it took to complete all of this, the church had the land prayed for and the money in the bank for improvements. At each breakthrough, everyone was so happy about what God had done they could have stopped praying and failed to move on. Instead, God gave them the vision, faith, and perseverance to keep trusting and see how He would move strategically to accomplish what was actually a rather complex plan. It is easy to think you have prayed enough when you see part of the answer. How much better it is to keep on praying until God is finished with His exceeding work.

Second Example

Another example occurred a few years ago in the southeastern part of the United States. The visionary pastor contacted the author to assist in developing a strategic plan for the church. A series of structured meetings were held which included the pastor, his staff, and elders. Slowly but surely the group began to understand the philosophy and process of strategic planning. Various committees worked on identifying purpose/mission/vision for the church. Other committees were formed for environmental analysis, strengths and weaknesses, and assumptions. The work of these committees set the stage for discussions on objectives and strategy.

The planning committee determined a good objective would be to grow by 1,000 members over the next three years. Major problems were financial resources, space, parking, and lack of facilities. The committee could also see the need to expand the church school. As usual, finances just were not there to handle the various building projects. All through the process there was continued prayer. There was a can-do spirit by all involved.

One member of the environmental analysis committee in charge of gathering a wide range of facts discovered plans to expand a major north-south state road to a national expressway—public information, but few in the area were aware of it.

The church property was on the northwest corner of a busy intersection a few miles east of the proposed expressway. Over the years the pastor had inquired about property on two of the other corners. Serious negotiations started as part of the planning committee work. An option to buy was negotiated for two of the intersection corners. A sizeable down payment that stretched the church's finances was made. If the church did not exercise the option within the time frame the down payment would be lost. What the planning committee was banking on was the increased value of the property due to the highway expansion.

Many in the church congregation were skeptical. The planning committee had planned and prayed and prayed some more. Everyone, including the author, felt a confirmation in their spirit it was the right thing to do.

The highway expansion went on as planned. Strip malls, gas stations, and other commercial ventures began at a rapid pace. A few miles to the east the church property value was going up. They exercised their options and bought both properties. Shortly thereafter, they sold one of the corner lots for cash. The money from the sale paid off the other lot, expanded the church, put in a new parking lot, provided for school expansion, and bought robes for the choir. That church continues today to meet its purpose/mission/vision.

Conclusion

Where did strategy end and the Spirit begin? The answer remains unclear. A combination of what we know about planning and organization was used. Every step of the way fervent prayer took place for guidance, the Lord's will, and the struggle to make the right decision.

Biblically Based Analysis of Planning and Management Principles

Introduction

What does the Bible say about planning? The Holy Spirit helps us know God's will and actions that are anointed. We do our best, then ask God for His best. My spirit confirms when the right plan is in the will of God. Nothing in this article is meant to imply that the Lord is to be left out.

> *"A plan in the heart of man is like deep water."—Proverbs 20:5 (paraphrased)*

> *"For which one of you when he wants to build a tower does not sit down and calculate the cost?"—Luke 14:28 (paraphrased)*

> *"Through wisdom is an house builded; and by understanding it is established."Proverbs 24:3*

> *"For God is not the author of confusion, but of peace. . ."— 1 Corinthians 14:33*

> *"Let all things be done decently and in order." —1 Corinthians 14:33*

Biblical/Management Comparison

Planning, roughly defined, is the process of looking to the future and determining how to get there. "The planning model for this article has been used successfully in businesses, churches, non-profit organizations, hospitals, government, and athletic managements." (1)

The model for the planning process is in Figure I.

Figure I Illustrates the Strategic Planning/MBO Process

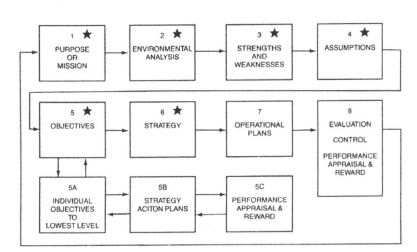

Purpose, Mission, Vision

Every organization needs to have a mission statement. Note two mission statements of manufacturing companies with a strong Christian base.

CROSS MANUFACTURING, INC.
MISSION STATEMENT

Through the design, production, and marketing of a complete line of fluid power products for both domestic and international markets, Cross Manufacturing, Inc., exists:

To make more money, both now and in the future by meeting needs in the marketplace, i.e., serving our customers with quality products, on-time deliveries, and competitive pricing; and, at the same time;

To glorify God by reflecting Christ in every business transaction, i.e., follow basic Biblical principles: honesty, integrity, honor others, be dependable, be fair, patient, and consistent. Provide value in the product. Treat suppliers, employees, and customers fairly. Provide a safe, ethical, discrimination-free environment for our employees. (4)

CARDONE INDUSTRIES, INC.
STATEMENT OF PURPOSE

We are in business to realize a profit for the mutual benefit of our employees, our customers, our suppliers, the community, and our owners.

Our corporate objectives are:

1. To honor God in all we do.

2. To help people develop.

3. To pursue excellence.

4. To grow profitably.

To this end, we pledge ourselves.

Our business is the Remanufacturing of Automobile Parts to serve the Automotive After-market.

Mission Statement: To be the best remanufacturer in the world.

We are in business:

1. To be customer driven.

2. To serve this market with the finest quality products at savings in cost over new parts, the most responsive fill service, and to make the Cardone line the highest profitable Remanufactured line for our customers.

3. To contribute to the conservation of America's natural energy and mineral resources through our recycling process.

4. To offer our customers the greatest possible profit potential.

Our intent is to provide our Cardone Family Members with a safe, healthy, comfortable working environment, to be equal opportunity employers, to encourage a holistic family atmosphere in our working relationships, to make clear that everyone is an equal, to encourage the development of people through training and to instill the belief that everyone is part of a viable, unified team and part of The Cardone Family.

Cardone Industries is committed to conducting its business relationships in the highest ethical standards as to be a credit to God, its owners, our employees, their families, our customers, our suppliers, and the community. Each, through a separate entity, is part of one unified family and the mutual benefit of the whole is achieved as the needs of one another are responded to.

Our intent is to be the leader in Market Share for each new immature line while selectively maintaining market share on mature product lines and at the same time maintaining our position as a low cost producer of remanufactured products. Our intent is to build long-term lasting relationships and maintain a servanthood position with each customer and supplier. We believe in servant leadership as the most effective way to lead.

Our position is that of a pioneer and proud leader in the automotive remanufacturing industry. Realizing we are accountable to God to be good stewards of all the resources He has entrusted to us, we are therefore committed to the highest level of efficiency in every operation. We are one, with the help of God, in constant pursuit of excellence. We firmly believe that . . . If you want a long and satisfying life . . . never forget to be truthful and kind . . . if you want favor with both God and man, and a reputation for good judgment and common sense, then trust the Lord completely . . . In everything you do, put God first, and He will direct you and crown your efforts with success.

Selections from the Bible: Proverbs 3, The Living Bible (3)

"For lack of guidance a nation (or in our case 'a person') falls, but many advisors make victory sure."— Proverbs 11:14 (NIV)

"Plans fail for lack of counsel, but with many advisers they succeed."— Proverbs 15:22 (NIV)

"Every purpose is established by counsel. . ."— Proverbs 20:18

"He that handleth a matter wisely shall find good. . ."— Proverbs 16:20

"Where there is no vision, the people perish. . ."— Proverbs 29:18

"As a man thinketh in his heart, so is he."— Proverbs 23:7 (paraphrased)

". . . Your old men shall dream dreams, your young men shall see visions."— Joel 2:28— Acts 2:17 (Essentially the same as Joel 2:28)

"For by the grace given me I say to every one of you: Do not think of yourself more highly than you ought, but rather think of yourself with sober judgment, in accordance with the measure of faith God has given you."— Romans 12:3 (NIV)

"If anyone thinks he is something when he is nothing, he deceives himself. Each one should test his own actions. Then he can take pride in himself, without comparing himself to somebody else. . ."— Galatians 6:34 (NIV)

". . . I urge you to live a life worthy of the calling you have received."— Ephesians 4:1 (NIV)

"Delight yourself in the Lord and he will give you the desires of your heart."— Psalm 37:4 (NIV)

"But seek first his kingdom and his righteousness, and all these things will be given to you as well."— Matthew 6:33 (NIV)

Environmental Analysis

Every organization must monitor the outside environment, what is going on in the market place. External factors must be considered in developing a plan.

"It is the glory of God to conceal a thing: but the honour of kings is to search out a matter."— Proverbs 25:2

"A prudent man forseeth the evil, and hideth himself: but the simple pass on, and are punished."— Proverbs 22:3

Strengths and Weaknesses

A well thought-out plan recognizes organization strengths and weaknesses. The organization takes advantage of its strengths and tries to correct weaknesses.

"To whom much is given, much is required."— Luke 12:48 (paraphrased)

". . . Complete and proficient, well-fitted and thoroughly equipped for every good work."— 2 Timothy 3:17 (AMP)

Objectives

Objectives are the measurable expected results of your plan. What are you shooting for? Objectives are specific and measurable in a time frame. Evelyn Roberts makes a major point and helps us understand objectives.

> *"For what dost thou make request? . . ." (What do you want?)— Nehemiah 2:4*

Strategy

Strategy is the game plan to achieve objectives.

> *"Neither do people light a lamp and put it under a bowl. Instead they put it on its stand, and it gives light to everyone in the house."— Matthew 5:15 (paraphrased)*

Operational Plan

Finally action must take place. Once developed, the plan must be implemented.

> *"Study to shew thyself approved unto God, a workman that needeth not to be ashamed. . ."— 2 Timothy 2:15*

> *". . . Complete and proficient, well-fitted and thoroughly equipped for every good work."— 2 Timothy 3:17 (AMP)*

> *"For which one of you when he wants to build a tower does not sit down and calculate the cost?"— Luke 14:28 (paraphrased)*

> *"For if any be a hearer of the word, and not a doer, he is like unto a man beholding his natural face in a glass."— James 1:23*

> *"Let all things be done decently and in order."— 1 Corinthians 14:40*

> *"For a great door and effectual is opened unto me, and there are many adversaries."— 1 Corinthians 16:9*

> *"I can do all things through Christ which strengtheneth me."— Philippians 4:13*

> *"And whatsoever ye do in word or deed, do all in the name of the Lord Jesus. . ."— Colossians 3:17*

> *"We should make plans—counting on God to direct us."— Proverbs 16:9 (TLB)*

> *"Commit thy works unto the Lord. . ."— Proverbs 16:3*

"Whatever you do, work at it with all your heart, as working for the Lord, not for men."— Colossians 3:23 (NIV)

". . . For what dost thou make request? So I prayed to the God of heaven."— Nehemiah 2:4

Reward

A good planning process provides both extrinsic and intrinsic rewards for all members of the organization.

"Now he who plants and he who waters are one; but each will receive his own reward according to his own labor."— 1 Corinthians 3:8 (paraphrased)

". . . The righteous will be rewarded with prosperity."— Proverbs 13:21 (paraphrased)

"I press toward the mark for the prize of the high calling of God in Christ Jesus."— Philippians 3:14

Plan in General

"Plans fail for lack of counsel, but with many advisers they succeed." — Proverbs 15:22 (NIV)

"A divine sentence is in the lips of the king: his mouth transgresseth not in judgment."— Proverbs 16:10

"Hear counsel and receive instruction, that thou mayest be wise. . ."— Proverbs 19:20

"A plan in the heart of a man is like deep water."— Proverbs 20:5 (paraphrased)

"Through wisdom is an house builded; and by understanding it is established."— Proverbs 24:3

"For God is not the author of confusion, but of peace. . ."— 1 Corinthians 14:33

Biblical Backup to Planning and Management

"Commit your work to the Lord, then it will succeed."; "Any enterprise is built by wise planning."— Proverbs 16:3, 24:3 (TLB)

"May he grant you your heart's desire and fulfill all your plans."— Psalm 20:4 (TLB)

"The Lord Almighty has sworn, Surely, as I have planned, so it will be, and as I have purposed, so it will stand."— Isaiah 14:24, 25 (NIV)

". . . What I have planned, that will I do. . ."— Isaiah 46:11

"Where there is no vision, the people perish: but he that keepeth the law, happy is he."— Proverbs 29:18

". . . And your young men shall see visions, and your old men shall dream dreams."— Acts 2:17

Conclusion

The logical conclusion is that the model of planning presented in this article has a Biblical base. Organization leaders can identify these steps and be confident there is a spiritual base. The two family-owned businesses, Cardone Industries, Inc., and Cross Manufacturing, Inc., introduced in the "Purpose" portion of this article are models of companies that not only have Christian values in their purpose statement, but practice what they preach. Can the organization make an honorable profit and prosper using Christian Biblical principles? Both Cardone and Cross remain profitable. Both companies plant profits into worthy causes.

The success of these two companies is well documented. Cardone Industries is highlighted in the article "A Family that Doesn't Fear the Dirty Work," (4) which covers the success of the company. Cross Manufacturing (5) received the very prestigious Ernst & Young Entrepreneur of the Year Award in the Turnaround Category. Both of these companies use the model in Figure I as the basis for their planning. Finally, it can be concluded that Biblical principles can be used and will contribute to the success of a for-profit enterprise.

References

Migliore, R. Henry, Strategic Planning for the New Millennium (Tulsa: Global Publishing, Sept. 2000).

Purpose Statement from Cross Manufacturing, Inc.

Purpose Statement from Cardone Industries, Inc.

"A Family Doesn't Fear the Dirty Work," *Philadelphia Business Journal 19*, no. 18 (June 9-15, 2000).

"Cross to Bear," *Johnson County Business Times,* (October 6, 1999): 10.

Common Sense Management. A Biblical Perspective

Care and Feeding of The Boss: Our attitude toward authority.

> *. . . make my joy complete by being like-minded, having the same love, being one in spirit and purpose. Do nothing out of selfish ambition or vain conceit, but in humility consider others better than yourselves. Each of you should look not only to your own interests, but also to the interests of others.—Philippians 2:2-4 NIV*

> *How good and pleasant it is when brothers (coworkers) live (and work) together in unity!—Psalm 133:1 NIV*

> *Anyone, then, who knows the good he ought to do and doesn't do it, sins.— James 4:17 NIV*

Care and Feeding of The Employee: How we treat those that report to us.

> *But this I say, He which soweth sparingly shall reap also sparingly; and he which soweth bountifully shall reap also bountifully.*

> *Now he that ministereth seed to the sower both minister bread for your food, and multiply your seed sown.—2 Corinthians 9:6, 10*

Iceberg Theory: Stay on the lookout for danger.

> *Only by pride cometh contention: but with the well advised is wisdom.— Proverbs 13:10*

> *Without counsel purposes are disappointed: but in the multitude of counselors they are established.—Proverbs 15:22*

> *A wise man sees danger; the fool goes his merry way.—Proverbs 22:3*

> *Hear counsel, and receive instruction, that thou mayest be wise in thy latter end.—Proverbs 19:20*

> *Every purpose is established by counsel. . .—Proverbs 20:18*

> *For by wise counsel thou shalt make thy war: and in multitude of counselors there is safety.—Proverbs 24:6*

Promotion Theory: Train your replacement, help others develop.

Think about:

> *Moses and Joshua*
> *Elijah and Elisha*
> *Paul and Timothy*

Jesus and the 12 Disciples

Managing Is Like Parenting: Be a responsible manager.

Train up a child in the way he should go (and in keeping with his individual gift or bent), and when he is old he will not depart from it.—Proverbs 22:6

Stinger Principle: Sometimes Christians must tackle problems head on.

Do not hold back discipline from the child, although you beat him with the rod, he will not die.

You shall beat him with the rod, and deliver his soul from Sheol.—Proverbs 23:13, 14 NAS

Correct your son, and he will give you comfort; he will also delight your soul.—Proverbs 29:17 NAS

Cycle Theory: What goes around comes around.

Let your eyes look right on (with fixed purpose), and let your gaze be straight before you.

Consider well the path of your feet, and let all your ways be established and ordered aright.—Proverbs 4:25, 26 AMP

Accordingly then, let us not sleep, as the rest do, but let us keep wide awake (alert, watchful, cautious, and on our guard) and let us be sober (calm, collected, and circumspect).—1 Thessalonians 5:6 AMP

But test and prove all things [until you can recognize] what is good; [to that] hold fast.—1 Thessalonians 5:21 AMP

Let me warn you therefore, beloved, that knowing these things beforehand, you should be on your guard lest you be carried away by the error of lawless and wicked (persons and) fall from your own (present) firm condition & your own steadfastness (of mind).—2 Peter 3:17 AMP

Pay Me Now, or Pay Me Later: Do it right the first time.

By wisdom a house is built, and through understanding it is established.—Proverbs 24:3 NIV

A tyrannical ruler lacks judgment.—Proverbs 28:16 NIV

A prudent man sees danger and takes refuge, but the simple keep going and suffer for it.—Proverbs 22:3 NIV

Afraid to Fail: Like the Nike commercial says, "Go for it."

> When you go to war against your enemies and see horses and chariots and an army greater than yours, do not be afraid of them because the Lord your God, who brought you up out of Egypt, will be with you. . .—Deuteronomy 20:1 NIV

> The steps of a good man are ordered by the Lord: and he delighteth in his way.—Psalm 37:23

Defensive End Theory: Get tough if you have to.

> Finally, my brethren, be strong in the Lord, and in the power of his might.—Ephesians 6:10

> If thou faint in the day of adversity, thy strength is small.—Proverbs 24:10

Alamo Theory—Toe the Line: Make sure everyone is heading in the right direction.

> He who scorns instruction will pay for it, but he who respects a command is rewarded.—Proverbs 13:13 NIV

> Then Moses stood in the gate of the camp, and said, Who is on the Lord's side? let him come unto me. . .—Exodus 32:26

> A servant cannot be corrected by mere words; though he understands, he will not respond.—Proverbs 29:19 NIV

> He who listens to a life-giving rebuke will be at home among the wise.—Proverbs 15:31 NIV

> A rebuke impresses a man of discernment more than a hundred lashes a fool.—Proverbs 17:10 NIV

Lawn-Mowing Theory: There is a way to get organized — each does what they do best.

> The eye cannot say to the hand, "I don't need you!" And the head cannot say to the feet, "I don't need you!" On the contrary, those parts of the body that seem to be weaker are indispensable.—1 Corinthians 12:21, 22 NIV

> Behold, how good and how pleasant it is for brethren to dwell together in unity!—Psalm 133:1

View the World Through (Other) Colored Glasses: Respect the view of others.

> *And if I have the gift of prophecy, and know all mysteries and all knowledge; and if I have all faith, so as to remove mountains, but do not have love, I am nothing.—1 Corinthians 13:2 NAS*

> *But now God has placed the members, each one of them, in the body, just as He desired.*

> *And if they were all one member, where would the body be?—1 Corinthians 12:18, 19 NAS*

Stew in Your Own Juice: Better get your team with you.

> *But I did not want to do anything without your consent, so that any favor you do will be spontaneous and not forced.—Philemon 14 NIV*

> *. . . He which soweth sparingly shall reap also sparingly.—2 Corinthians 9:6a*

> *Be not deceived; God is not mocked: for whatsoever a man soweth, that shall he also reap.—Galatians 6:7*

Snowball: Things, events, a course of action can get out of control.

> *Now finish the work so that your eager willingness to do it may be matched by your completion of it, according to your means.—2 Corinthians 8:11 NIV*

Get Your Head Above the Clouds: Take a look where you are going.

> *In all thy ways acknowledge him, and he shall direct thy paths.—Proverbs 3:6*

> *A man's heart deviseth his way: but the Lord directeth his steps.—Proverbs 16:9*

Homeostasis: Be aware that there is an integration — cause — effect. We have both: We effect and affect others.

> *. . . If as one people speaking the same language they have begun to do this, then nothing they plan to do will be impossible for them.—Genesis 11:6 NIV*

> *Do not conform any longer to the pattern of this world, but be transformed by the renewing of your mind. Then you will be able to test and approve what God's will is — his good, pleasing and perfect will.—Romans 12:2 NIV*

Seed Faith: Better to give than receive.

> *Give, and it shall be given unto you; good measure, pressed down, and shaken together, and running over, shall men give into your bosom. For with the same measure that ye mete withal it shall be measured to you again.— Luke 6:38*

Natural Rhythm: There is a rhythm to everything.

> *Except the Lord build the house, they labour in vain that build it.—Psalm 127:1a*

> *This book of the law shall not depart from your mouth, but you shall meditate on it day and night, so that you may be careful to do according to all that is written in it: for then you will make your way prosperous, and then you will have success.—Joshua 1:8 NAS*

> *To every thing there is a season, and a time to every purpose under the heaven:*

> *A time to be born, and a time to die; a time to plant, and a time to pluck up that which is planted;*

> *A time to kill, and a time to heal; a time to break down, and a time to build up;*

> *A time to weep, and a time to laugh; a time to mourn, and a time to dance;*

> *A time to cast away stones, and a time to gather stones together; a time to embrace, and a time to refrain from embracing;*

> *A time to get, and a time to lose; a time to keep, and a time to cast away;*

> *A time to rend, and a time to sew; a time to keep silence, and a time to speak;*

> *A time to love, and a time to hate; a time of war, and a time of peace.*

> *—Ecclesiastes 3:1-8*

I'll Be True to You While You're Gone, Honey . . . Just Don't Be Gone Too Long": *Don't forget your friends and family.*

> *Be hospitable to one another without complaint.*

> *As each one has received a special gift, employ it in serving one another, as good stewards of the manifold grace of God.—1 Peter 4:9, 10 NAS*

Find Out He is a Christian by How He Acts, Not by What He Says: Actions speak louder than words.

> *Let your light so shine before men, that they may see your good works, and glorify your Father which is in heaven.—Matthew 5:16*

> *Yea, a man may say, Thou hast faith, and I have works: shew me thy faith without thy works, and I will shew thee my faith by my works.—James 2:18*

> *Having your conversation honest among the Gentiles: that, whereas they speak against you as evildoers, they may by your good works, which they shall behold, glorify God in the day of visitation.—1 Peter 2:12*

Be the Best You Can Be: Don't give the Lord second best.

> *And whatever you do in word or deed, do all in the name of the Lord Jesus, giving thanks through Him to God the Father.—Colossians 3:17 NAS*

> *Finally then, brethren, we request and exhort you in the Lord Jesus, that, as you received from us instruction as to how you ought to walk and please God (just as you actually do walk), that you may excel still more.—1 Thessalonians 4:1 NAS*

Never Give Up: Just keep plugging.

> *Do you not know that those who run in a race all run, but only one receives the prize? Run in such a way that you may win.—1 Corinthians 9:24 NAS*

Do It When It Is Important: We tend to put things off.

> *Withhold not good from them to whom it is due, when it is in the power of thine hand to do it.*

> *Say not unto thy neighbor, Go, and come again, and to morrow I will give; when thou hast it by thee.—Proverbs 3:27, 28*

Success of The Whole Person: Success is broader than your career.

> *Dear friend, I pray that you may enjoy good health and that all may go well with you, even as your soul is getting along well.—3 John 2 NIV*

> *Do not wear yourself out to get rich; have the wisdom to show restraint.— Proverbs 23:4 NIV*

Be There in the Morning: Be loyal to the cause.

> *Most men will proclaim every one his own goodness: but a faithful man who can find?—Proverbs 20:6*

> *Who then is a faithful and wise servant, whom his lord hath made ruler over his household, to give them meat in due season?*

> *Blessed is that servant, whom his lord when he cometh shall find so doing.— Matthew 24:45, 46*

Failing to Prepare Is Like Preparing to Fail

> *For lack of guidance a nation falls, but many advisers make victory sure.— Proverbs 11:14 NIV*

The Product Must be Better Than the Sales Pitch

> *Oral Roberts, former President of Oral Roberts University, made this statement at the beginning of a School of Business Marketing Conference at ORU. He was referring to Jesus and the message to the business audience was that "their product must be better than the sales pitch."*

The O-Ring

> *For lack of guidance a nation falls, but many advisers make victory sure.— Proverbs 11:14 NIV*

> *Plans fail for lack of counsel, but with many advisers they succeed.—Proverbs 15:22 NIV*

> *Listen to advice and accept instruction, and in the end you will be wise.— Proverbs 19:20 NIV*

Scriptures Relating to Promotion Theory

The Great Commission

And Jesus came and spake unto them, saying, All power is given unto me in heaven and in earth.

Go ye therefore, and teach all nations, baptizing them in the name of the Father, and of the Son, and of the Holy Ghost:

Teaching them to observe all things whatsoever I have commanded you: and, lo, I am with you always, even unto the end of the world. Amen.

—Matthew 28:18-20

Elijah and Elisha

So he (Elijah) departed thence, and found Elisha the son of Shaphat, who was plowing with twelve yoke of oxen before him, and he with the twelfth: and Elijah passed by him, and cast his mantle upon him.

And he left the oxen, and ran after Elijah, and said, Let me, I pray thee, kiss my father and my mother, and then I will follow thee. And he said unto him, Go back again: for what have I done to thee?

And he returned back from him, and took a yoke of oxen, and slew them, and boiled their flesh with the instruments of the oxen, and gave unto the people, and they did eat. Then he arose, and went after Elijah, and ministered unto him.

—*I Kings 19:19-21*

. . . Elijah said unto Elisha, Ask what I shall do for thee, before I be taken away from thee. And Elisha said, I pray thee, let a double portion of thy spirit be upon me.

And he said, Thou has asked a hard thing: nevertheless, if thou see me when I am taken from thee, it shall be so unto thee; but if not, it shall not be so.

And it came to pass, as they still went on, and talked, that, behold, there appeared a chariot of fire, and horses of fire, and parted them both asunder; and Elijah went up by a whirlwind into heaven.

And Elisha saw it, and he cried, My father, my father, the chariot of Israel, and the horsemen thereof. And he saw them no more: and he took hold of his own clothes, and rent them in two pieces.

He took up also the mantel of Elijah that fell from him, and went back, and stood by the bank of Jordan;

And he took the mantle of Elijah that fell from him, and smote the waters, and said, Where is the Lord God of Elijah? and when he also had smitten the waters, they parted hither and thither: and Elisha went over.

And when the sons of the prophets which were to view at Jericho saw him, they said, The spirit of Elijah doth rest on Elisha. And they came to meet him, and bowed themselves to the ground before him.

—*II Kings 2:9-15*

The Calling of the First Disciples

And Jesus, walking by the sea of Galilee, saw two brethren, Simon called Peter, and Andrew his brother, casting a net into the sea: for they were fishers.

And he saith unto them, Follow me, and I will make you fishers of men.

And they straightway left their nets, and followed him.

And going on from thence, he saw other two brethren, James the son of Zebedee, and John his brother, in a ship with Zebedee their father, mending their nets; and he called them.

And they immediately left the ship and their father, and followed him.
—*Matthew 4:18-22*

Wisdom is the principal thing: therefore get wisdom: and with all thy getting get understanding.

Exalt her, and she shall promote thee: she shall bring thee to honor, when thou dost embrace her.—Proverbs 4:7-8

R. HENRY MIGLIORE, PhD, is a leading strategist for long-term planning for business, sports, and religious leaders. He offers consulting services as well as resources including books, videos, articles, seminars, and training sessions.

He is currently the president of Managing for Success, an international consulting company. Dr. Migliore teaches at the graduate and undergraduate levels at universities worldwide. He was Professor of Management and former Dean of the ORU School of Business from 1975 until 1987. From 1887 to 2003 he was Facet Enterprises Professor of Management at UCT/'NSU Tulsa. From 2003 to date he has worked worldwide as author, visiting professor and consultant. He is currently assisting ORU Global Outreach Center with broadcasts to various target markets worldwide.

He is a former manager of the press manufacturing operations of the Continental Can Company's Stockyard Plant. Prior to that he was responsible for the industrial engineering function at Continental's Indiana plant. In this capacity, Dr. Migliore was responsible for coordinating the long-range planning process. In addition, he has had various consulting experiences with Fred Rudge & Associates in New York and has served large and small businesses, associations, and non-profit organizations in various capacities.

He has made presentations to a wide variety of clubs, groups, and professional associations. Dr. Migliore has been selected to be on the faculty for the International Conferences on Management by Objectives and Strategic Planning Institute Seminar Series and he is a frequent contributor to the Academy of Management. He served for 12 years on the Board of Directors of T.D. Williamson, Inc., and was previously on the Boards of the International MBO Institute and Brush Creek Ranch, American Red Cross/Tulsa Chapter, and is chairman of a scholarship fund for Eastern State College. In 1984, he was elected into the Eastern State College Athletic Hall of Fame. Dr. Migliore has been a guest lecturer on a number of college campuses, including Harvard, Texas A&M, Pepperdine, ITESM, Guadalajara, Autonoma De Guadalajara, and University of Calgary Executive Development programs. He serves on many chamber and civic committees. He was selected Who's Who on a list of 31 top echelon writers and consultants in America.

Dr. Migliore's books have been translated into Russian, Chinese, Korean, Spanish, German, and Japanese.

He has 17 books in total. His next book in process is *Fourth Quarter Redefined*.

R. HENRY MIGLIORE, PhD

PRESIDENT OF MANAGING FOR SUCCESS

10839 SOUTH HOUSTON • JENKS, OK 74037 • (918) 299-0007

EMAIL: HMIGLIORE@AOL.COM

WEBSITE: WWW.HMIGLIORE.COM • YOUTUBE: DRMIGLIORE

Index

Symbols

1 Corinthians
  3:8: 86, 138
    9:24: 145
  12:18, 19: 143
  12:21, 22: 142
  13:2: 143
  14:33: 9, 133, 138
  14:40: 8, 15, 84, 85, 137
  16:9: 137
1 Peter
  2:12: 145
  4:9, 10: 144
1 Thessalonians
  4:1: 145
  5:6: 141
  5:21: 141
2 Corinthians
  8:11: 143
  9:6, 10: 140
  9:6a: 143
2 John
  1:8: 75
2 Peter
  3:17: 141
2 Timothy
  2:15: 86, 137
  3:17: 83, 136, 137
3 John
  2: 145

A

Acts
  2:17: 139
  2:42: 30
alternate strategies, 65–67
  differentiated, 66
  focus, 67
American Resource Bureau, 39
Analysis and Assumptions Worksheet 45
attendance control, 77–78

C

Cable Connections for Christ, 39–40
Calvary Temple, 93–100
Cardone Industries, Inc., 134–135
Case Study, 121–130
Christ Is The Answer, 68

church, 42
  assessing strengths and weaknesses, 42–43
church administrator's objectives, 61–62
Colossians
  3:17: 137, 145
  3:23: 9, 138
constituent feedback, 79
contribution/cost controls, 78–79
Cross Manufacturing, Inc., 134

D

Deuteronomy
  20:1: 142

E

Ecclesiastes
  3:1-8: 144
Ephesians
  4:1: 136
  6:10: 142
establishing procedures, 79
Evaluation and Control Worksheet, 80–81
Exodus
  32:26: 142
external analysis, 39–40
  making assumptions, 43–45
  opportunities and threats, 40–41

F

First Baptist Church of West Monroe, 66–67

G

Galatians
  6:7: 143
  6:34: 136
Genesis
  11:6: 143
greatest needs of ministries and churches,
    10–12

H

Holy Spirit, 8, 30, 44, 133

I

II Kings
  2:9-15: 147
I Kings

19:19-21: 147
Inner City Marketing Plan, 101–109
internal analysis, 41–42
Isaiah
14:24, 25: 139
46:11: 139

J

James
1:23: 137
2:18: 145
4:17: 140
Joel
2:28: 83, 136
Joshua
1:8: 144

L

lack of management training, 7–8
laws of organization
first law, 121–122
forces of, 128–130
second law, 127
third law, 127
Lindgren, Alvin J. 5
Luke
6:38: 144
12:48: 83, 136
14:28: 8, 86, 133, 137

M

managing by crisis, 49
managing by extrapolation , 48–49
managing by hope, 49
managing by subjectives , 49
marketing, 87
general marketing strategy, 87–88
purpose of marketing function, 87
Matthew
4:18-22: 148
5:15: 85, 137
5:16: 145
6:33: 136
24:45, 46: 146
28:18-20: 146
mission statement, 134
Missions to Mexico, 67
Morris Cerullo World Evangelism, 35

N

Nehemiah
2:4: 84, 137, 138

O

objectives, 20, 47
characteristics of good objectives, 50–53
classification of, 48
definition of, 48
fundamental purposes of, 48
nature and role of, 47–48
setting, 56–57
types of, 53–56
attendance, 53
constituent, 55–57
contribution, 54–55
worksheet, 62–63
operational plans, 21, 68–72
overall church objectives, 58–60

P

pastors, 1–2, 5–7, 10–11, 129
performance contracts, 57
performance evaluation and control, 77
performance evaluation guidelines, 79–80
periodic review, 57–58
Philemon
14: 143
Philippians
2:2-4: 140
3:14: 47, 138
4:13: 137
planning
advantages of, 4–6
as unscriptural, 8–9
definition, 3–4
implementation problems, 9–10
importance of, 1–3
long-range, 6
place in the church or ministry, 7
reasons for, 6–7
resistance to, 7–9
planning and control
integration of, 75–77
Proverbs
3:6: 143
3:27, 28: 145
4:7-8: 148
4:25, 26: 141

11:14: 146
11:14: (NIV) 135
13:10: 140
13:13: 142
13:21: 138
15:22: 9, 135, 138, 140, 146
15:31: 142
16:3: 1, 8, 137, 138
16:9: 8, 137, 143
16:10: 138
16:20: 135
17:10: 142
18:22: 16
19:20: 17, 138, 140, 146
20:4: 65
20:5: 9, 133, 138
20:6: 146
20:8: 17
20:18: 135, 140
22:3: 136, 140, 141
22:6: 141
23:4: 145
23:7: 136
23:13, 14: 141
24:3: 9, 133, 138, 141
24:6: 140
24:10: 142
25:2: 39, 83, 136
28:16: 141
29:8: 27
29:17: 141
29:18: 83, 136, 139
29:19: 142
Psalm 9
  20:4: 9, 138
  37:4: 136
  37:23: 142
  127:1a: 144
  133:1: 140, 142
purpose statement
  congregational care, 29
  defining, 27–28
  evaluating, 34–35
  outreach and evangelism, 29
  witness and mission, 29
  worksheet, 37
  writing a statement of, 28–29

R

review sheet management plan, 60–61
Robertson, Pat, 39

Romans
  12:2: 143
  12:3: 136

S

sample mission statements, 29–34
  Asbury Theological Seminary, 31–34
  Monroe Covenant Church, 29–31
small churches, 5, 128
Strategic and Management Planning Work-
    sheets, 83–86
strategic planning
  analysis and assumptions, 19–20
  and Spirit, 130–133
  as a process, 22
  defining purpose, 18–19
  definition, 15
  establishing objectives, 20
  evaluation and control, 21
  implementation, 22
  process, 15–18
  steps, 17–18
strategy concepts, 65
strategy selectionfactors influencing, 67
SWOT 19

T

the two Ps, 16

V

Victory Christian Center, 35

W

Wesley, John, 35